ST. MARY'S COLL
ST. MARY

S0-AJE-943

Abraham Lincoln

BY SOME MEN WHO KNEW HIM

37107

Abraham Lincoln
BY SOME MEN WHO KNEW HIM

Being Personal Recollections of

JUDGE OWEN T. REEVES
HON. JAMES S. EWING
COL. RICHARD P. MORGAN
JUDGE FRANKLIN BLADES
JOHN W. BUNN

★

With Introduction by

HON. ISAAC N. PHILLIPS

★

Edited with Notes and Foreword by

PAUL M. ANGLE

Essay Index Reprint Series

BOOKS FOR LIBRARIES PRESS
FREEPORT, NEW YORK

Copyright, 1950, by Americana House
Reprinted 1969 by arrangement
with Abraham Lincoln Book Shop

STANDARD BOOK NUMBER:
8369-1242-X

LIBRARY OF CONGRESS CATALOG CARD NUMBER:
78-90601

PRINTED IN THE UNITED STATES OF AMERICA

TO THOSE WHO HAVE READ VOLUMES

OF LINCOLN BIOGRAPHIES

IN A VAIN EFFORT

TO FORM A CORRECT ESTIMATE OF

LINCOLN, THE MAN, THIS BOOK

IS RESPECTFULLY DEDICATED.

FOREWORD

IT IS APPARENT, *from the original editor's Introduction, that this book owes its existence to the Lincoln Centenary. Three of the five reminiscences which it contains were speeches delivered at centennial gatherings. These are its nucleus, and without them, one may fairly surmise, it would never have come into being.*

What is more important is that the book also owes its character to the one hundredth anniversary of Lincoln's birth. The Centenary loosed a veritable flood of printer's ink. For months, in 1909, newspapers and magazines were filled with "Lincoln stories," while on three days out of four throughout the year a separate book or pamphlet came from the presses. Much of the outpouring was unrestrained eulogy.[1] Much was

---

[1] A typical sample: "Abraham Lincoln was so great, so noble, so grand, and so peerless a man that no man living, no matter how eloquent may be his tongue—no man living, no matter how gifted with the pen—no artist, regardless of his dexterity with the brush—no sculptor, notwithstanding the genius of his handicraft—will be able to portray, describe, paint or chisel that life-likeness of Lincoln, which his diverse and varied features and changing countenance evolved." Bernard J. Cigrand at the Chicago Commemoration of the Lincoln Centenary.

7

also so misinformed, so misconceived, as to be a biographical travesty. Small wonder that men who had known Lincoln feared that the real man was in danger of being lost forever.

Against this sort of thing Isaac N. Phillips revolted. Having lived at Bloomington, Illinois, since 1872, he was acquainted with many of Lincoln's old friends and associates, and the man about whom he had learned from them was not always recognizable in the effusions of 1909. Given an editorial assignment, he determined to put together a book in which the contributors would write no more than they knew. He had three centennial addresses that met his standard. To supplement these he induced two men of knowledge and good sense—Franklin Blades, once a member of the Illinois legislature, and John W. Bunn, Springfield merchant and banker—to write their recollections.

These five reminiscences, with Phillips's Introduction and biographical sketches, are all there is to Abraham Lincoln By Some Men Who Knew Him. *Let us admit that the book makes no weighty contribution to the history of the years with which it deals, and that such political analysis as is to be found in it was time-worn even in 1910. It reveals no facts of significance, and contains the usual quota of minor* errors. *Those who wrote it were worthy men, but not of sufficient reputation to make their writings interesting on the sole ground of authorship. What they had to say they said well, yet without real stylistic distinction.*

Nevertheless, it has appealed to so many readers that copies have long been difficult to come by. Why? Partly, I believe, because of its unpretentious sincerity. What could be more modest than its title? Only the disclaimer, by several of the contributors, of any closer knowledge of Lincoln than was possessed by hundreds of his contemporaries. They knew him as young men know an older man, already distinguished. They remembered episodes during the last years of his life in Illinois; they had vivid impressions of character and personality. These they recorded without embellishment and without any desire, as far as one can see, to shine in the reflected light of their acquaintanceship.

But in greater part the attraction of Abraham Lincoln By Some Men Who Knew Him comes from the success of its authors in developing a composite character sketch that carries conviction. A necessary part of that development was the clearing away of certain conceptions that still have some currency. Thus they reiterated that Lincoln was not the kind of man whom one

9

called "Abe," and denied, with heat, that he was "ill-mannered, uncouth, unrefined in sentiment, the indulger of vulgarity of speech, a buffoon and yarn-spinner." On the contrary, they portrayed him as simple, humorous, friendly, yet reserved, resolute, sagacious, and with great depths of human sympathy—in short, as a character wholly consonant with the greatness that mankind has attributed to him.

It is good that their testimony should again be available.

PAUL M. ANGLE

Preface to Original Edition

IN THE PUBLICATION of this unique little volume, we are justified by the fact that so much unreliable information has been published concerning Lincoln. We feel a laudable ambition to set right, so far as possible, erroneous impressions.

We have neither added to nor taken from, these personal recollections of honorable gentlemen who lived the life as Lincoln lived it, and who are, therefore, capable of arriving at a fairly accurate estimate of his true character.

THE PUBLISHERS

11

Introduction to Original Edition

I AM ASKED to write an introduction to this little book. I confess I feel a very considerable interest in the subject of it and am very glad to see it go forth to the world. The book represents a praiseworthy effort on the part of its publishers—The Pantagraph Printing & Stationery Company, of Bloomington, Illinois—to preserve in a permanent form some original evidence upon the question, "What kind of a man was Lincoln?"

I know very many people have of late been telling the world what kind of a man Lincoln was, and have been relating many incidents, facts and recollections concerning him. On the centenary of Lincoln's birth, the newspapers of the country were flooded with interviews and communications from all sorts of people. There are, in fact, very few men now living who knew Abraham Lincoln at all well, or who saw much of him, and who have at the same time definite personal recollections concerning him. The recollections here given are given by persons who, I know, really did know Lincoln. They are likewise persons who would not pretend to know things they do not know.

There were never more than a very few men who could at any time pretend to have been on terms at all intimate with Lincoln, because Lincoln took but few, if any, into his deeper confidences. The men whose recollections are given in this book do not pretend that they were on deeply confidential terms with Lincoln. Nobody living can now pretend to that, and the man who does pretend to it may be generally set down as mistaken. The men who speak here have some memories and recollections concerning Lincoln and they give us these memories for what they are worth.

It is useless to assure readers that the writer of this introduction would never have been active in helping to cause these recollections to be published, if he had not believed that they set forth the real truth, so far as they go, concerning Lincoln. These men were all quite close friends of my own. I know each of them to be a man who would not pervert the truth in order to make a mouthable or amusing story, and I further know that the memory of each of these gentlemen was, when he wrote, very distinct and clear.

I am exceedingly gratified to get this testimony

on record, where the future historian may find it, for we may be sure the real life of Lincoln has not yet been written, and, unless the confusion surrounding the subject shall clear up more rapidly than it bids fair to do, the real life of Lincoln will not be written for at least another fifty years. It will quite surely not be written before the generation of men who knew Lincoln in life are all dead and gone. It was so with Washington, and it is going to be so with Lincoln. Washington was so far perverted by would-be story tellers and biographers, that only the man who now studies Washington very carefully really knows what manner of man he was, and, sad to say, the men who study his life with care are now very few. In the early period, he was much belittled by busy-bodies who pretended to know all about him.

When preparations were in progress in Bloomington for the celebration of the centenary of Lincoln's birthday, being on a committee of the Grand Army Post of Bloomington which had in charge the selection of speakers, I insisted that men should be selected to speak who had a personal knowledge of Lincoln. We already had plenty of eulogies; what we needed was facts. I knew that the men who really had valuable information were apt to be modest men, who would

15

not rush forward to be interviewed or to make speeches. Two notable speeches that were made at the celebration on the afternoon of the 12th of February, 1909, namely, that of Hon. Adlai E. Stevenson and that of Judge Reuben M. Benjamin, both of Bloomington, have already been published in MacChesney's book, "The Tribute of A Century," and there appear under copyright. Another speech from the same platform and on the same occasion was made by Judge Owen T. Reeves, likewise of Bloomington and is included in this book. Another address setting forth some recollections of Lincoln was made on the evening of that day at Bloomington by Hon. James S. Ewing, before the Illinois Schoolmasters' Club, and that speech likewise is given in this book. At Pontiac, Illinois, where a like celebration was held on the same day, Colonel Richard Price Morgan, of Dwight, Ill., delivered an address, giving some recollections of Lincoln, and Col. Morgan's address is also printed here. At my special solicitation Judge Franklin Blades, of Pomona, California, wrote out his recollections of Lincoln, which will be found very interesting and are included here.

I venture to call special attention to the set of resolutions, written by Lincoln, and passed by the Illinois legislature in January, 1861, as re-

lated by Judge Blades. These have hitherto es-
caped attention. Judge Blades, I am proud to
say, has long been my personal friend. His testi-
mony on the question of the authorship of
these resolutions is absolutely conclusive. I know
him to be as conscientious a man as ever lived,
exceedingly careful not to state more than he
knows.

John W. Bunn, of Springfield, Illinois, is well
known to be about the last survivor in Spring-
field who knew Lincoln well before the war,
and, at my special solicitation, he has written
out some of his recollections of Lincoln, and it
is a great pleasure to me to present them in this
book. I regard Mr. Bunn as really the best au-
thority upon Lincoln in the period before the
Civil War.

Much has been said about Lincoln's supposed
propensity to spin yarns and tell doubtful anec-
dotes. That Lincoln was a sort of fabulist and
illustrated his points by incidents and remem-
bered happenings, is true, but biographers, and
particularly would-be "old familiar friends" have
so greatly over-stated Lincoln's story telling pro-
pensity that it is well that men who really knew
him well and can be relied upon to state facts,
should be heard on the subject.

Another class of writers have seemed exceed-

ingly anxious to make it appear that Lincoln came literally from nothing. The Bible tells us that men do not gather figs from thistles, but some of the biographers would have us believe that this saying of the Holy Writ does not apply to Lincoln. Many of them make a special point of belittling and discrediting his parents and ancestors in order to produce a striking contrast for the purpose of eulogy. Such persons are, in nearly every instance, animated more by a desire to attract attention to themselves than by a desire to really depict the great man who lived, worked and aspired, out here in Illinois, and who at last attained to the hard but glorious privilege of martyrdom for his cause.

ISAAC N. PHILLIPS

Biographical Sketch of
JUDGE OWEN T. REEVES

JUDGE OWEN T. REEVES *was born December 18,
1829, in Ross County, Ohio. He was graduated
from the Ohio Wesleyan University in 1850,
and three years later received from that University
the degree of Master of Arts. In 1888 he
received the degree of LL.D. from Monmouth
College, in Illinois. From 1850 to 1854 he was
engaged in teaching. He came to Bloomington,
Illinois, in October, 1854, which place has since
been his home. Judge Reeves was admitted to
the bar before leaving Ohio and commenced the
practice of law when he settled at Bloomington.
In 1861 he was appointed city clerk and city
attorney of Bloomington. He was elected a circuit judge March 1, 1877, and remained on the
bench until June, 1891. The last three years of
his judicial service he was, by assignment of the
Illinois Supreme Court, a judge of the Illinois
Appellate Court for the Fourth District. Since
1891 he has been Dean of the Bloomington Law
School. In the Civil War he was Colonel of the
70th Illinois Infantry. Judge Reeves was one of
the most impartial and most clear-headed judges
that ever held a nisi prius court, as the lawyers
who practiced before him will universally testify.*

Personal Recollections
and Estimates of Lincoln

OWEN T. REEVES

RECALL with marked distinctness my impressions on my first meeting Mr. Lincoln in March, 1855. I had heard much of him before I met him. His candidacy for the United States Senate before the General Assembly in January, 1855, had focused my attention upon him. The unusual complimentary comments by those who had known him many years—some of whom were directly opposed to him politically—riveted my attention to this unusual man. No wonder, then, that when I met him I was specially attracted to a careful analysis of how he impressed me, and that this analysis is still distinct in memory.

20

Speaking generally, I may say that I now recall clearly that I was deeply impressed with the fact that I had met a man widely different from the ordinary man of distinction. There was something, just what not clearly defined, in him, that stamped him in my conception as a man of marked superiority intellectually.

Lincoln's personality was to me a revelation, different from any other personality I had ever tried to measure and comprehend, although it had been my good fortune in prior years to have had personal relations with a goodly number of men of wide and well-merited distinction. He had an individuality that was singularly impressive. Altogether, the problem of his true measure as a man was complex and not easy of solution. To me Mr. Lincoln was a continuous study, and the farther the study was carried, the higher the estimate of him arose until, to me, he stood out as a veritable marvel among men.

From March, 1855, to the Spring of 1860, I met Mr. Lincoln often and became quite intimately acquainted with him. He attended all the sessions of the McLean County Circuit Court during that period. I heard him try many cases—some of large importance, and many ordinary cases. I recall his assisting the State's Attorney in the prosecution of one Wyatt for murder, a hard-fought case in which Leonard Swett succeeded in acquitting Wyatt of murder, on the ground of insanity. He appeared for plaintiff, Meshach Pike, in a suit to set aside the sale of the Pike Hotel at Bloomington, on the ground of fraud on the part of the purchaser. Judge T. L. Dickey, of Ottawa, and local attorneys appeared for the defense, and Lincoln won out. He defended a chancery suit in which I appeared for complainant, by which it was sought to set aside a sale of school lands, which resulted in favor of the defendant. He represented the Illinois Central Railroad Company in its suit, contesting the validity of an assessment by the county of McLean of county taxes against the railroad company, in which he was successful in defeating the tax. This suit settled the non-liability of the Illinois Central Railroad Company for local taxes for the full period of its charter.

Lincoln was engaged during this period in the trial of a great variety of cases, his employment being sufficient to maintain his presence in court practically during the entire sessions of the court.

It is not my purpose, in the brief time allotted me, to speak further of Lincoln as a lawyer. Referring to Lincoln's personal characteristics, I will say that to portray Lincoln as ill-mannered, uncouth, unrefined in sentiment, the indulger of vulgarity of speech, a buffoon and yarn-spinner, is a complete and outrageous caricature, as I knew him. His mind, in all its serious moods, which was its prevailing condition, was occupied by lofty thoughts upon subjects of the highest concern, developing a philosophy of life in all its myriad phases, based upon sound reason and exalted conceptions.

I heard Lincoln tell hundreds of anecdotes and stories, but never one that was not told to illustrate or give point to some subject or question that had been the theme of conversation, or that was not suggested by an anecdote or story told by someone else. This fact found an apt illustration, when Lincoln was asked what he thought of Hood's army after its sweeping defeat at the battle of Nashville, Tenn., by General Thomas. Lincoln said the question reminded him of the story of an Illinois farmer who had been sorely annoyed by a marauding dog. The farmer procured a piece of meat into which there was put a powerful explosive, and placed the meat in the path that the dog would take to reach the place where his usual depredations were committed. He tied a string, saturated with gasoline, to the piece of meat and took a position behind a tree from which he could see the dog as he approached. He fired the string in time to reach the meat at the same time as the dog. The result was the dog gulped the meat and instantly there was an explosion. When the farmer was asked what was the effect on the dog, he replied, "That dog, *as a dog,* will not ever again amount to much." So Lincoln's answer to the question asked him was, "I don't think Hood's army, *as an army,* will hereafter amount to much."

A short time ago, I came across a statement said to have been made by Lincoln, during the war, when challenged to tell a story. He said: "I believe I have the popular reputation of being a story-teller, but I do not deserve the name in any general sense; for it is not the story itself, but its purpose or effect, that interests me. I often avoid a long and useless discussion by others, or a laborious explanation on my own part, by a short story that illustrates my point of view. So, too, the sharpness of a refusal or the edge of a rebuke may be blunted by an appropriate story so as to save wounded feeling and yet serve the purpose. No, I am not simply a story-teller, but story-telling as an emollient saves me much friction and distress."

Lincoln was the apostle of the common people.

Their rights, their conditions, their hardships, their opportunities, their aspirations, their hopes, their joys, their sorrows—all these were subjects upon which his mind brooded and sought to work out plans for their betterment and happiness. No man I ever met knew the common people better than he, or was in closer sympathy with them. Having sprung from the innumerable common throng, his heart never ceased to beat in sympathy with them. Besides, he was endowed with that best sense—common sense. This, with his broad, clear grasp of every subject that touched the interests of the masses, made him pre-eminently the advocate of the rights of the common people.

Up to the time of the repeal of the Missouri Compromise in 1854, Lincoln had not become recognized as a great leader in matters of state. He had been active as a Whig on the stump, and had served one term in Congress, besides a number of terms in the legislature, but, practically, after the close of his term in Congress, he returned to the practice of law, and devoted himself almost exclusively to his profession. The repeal of the Missouri Compromise made quite an upheaval in political parties and started a new movement.

Lincoln at an early date became settled in

the conviction that human slavery was both in the abstract and concrete, morally wrong. While this conviction grew with the years, he recognized that slavery, as it existed in the Southern States, was protected by the Constitution, and any interference with slavery as it existed in the South was unwarranted and could not be supported *simply by a belief that it was wrong.* Hence, he refused to co-operate with what was known as the Abolition party, and had no sympathy with its doctrines. However, while this was true, he was always unalterably opposed to the extension of slavery into the territories. He had clearly worked out, in his consideration of the subject of slavery as it existed in the Southern States, that, so far as its continued existence there was involved, there was no power outside of those States to interfere with it, but while this was true and to be conscientiously observed, there was no reason why opposition might not be made to its extension into the territories of the United States.

Lincoln went a step farther in his speech at Springfield in June, 1858, in which he declared: "A house divided against itself cannot stand. I believe that this Government cannot endure permanently half-slave and half-free. I do not expect the Union to be dissolved—I do not ex-

pect the house to fall—but I do expect it will
cease to be divided. It will become all one thing
or all the other. Either the opponents of slavery
will arrest the further spread of it and place it
where the public mind shall rest in the belief
that it is in the course of ultimate extinction, or
its advocates will push it forward till it shall become alike lawful in all the States, old as well as
new, North as well as South."

This prediction of his was predicated upon
his belief that the conviction of the great wrong
of slavery would in time work out, in some way,
its extinction; either that or the opinions of men
would change as to the moral character of slavery, so that it would come into use the country
over—plainly his belief was that the sentiment
against slavery would not cease, but continue
to grow, and, eventually, would work out the
ultimate extinction of slavery.

Most naturally, with his deep-seated conviction on the subject of slavery, Lincoln at once
became absorbed in the questions which sprung
out of the repeal of the Missouri Compromise,
and he at once became a leader of the forces
that opposed this repeal. October third, 1854,
Douglas, at the State Fair in Springfield, made
his great speech in defense of the Kansas and
Nebraska bill which repealed the Missouri Com-

27

promise, and by which Judge Douglas introduced his doctrine of popular sovereignty, under
which the people in the territories were left to
decide whether they would have slavery or not.
October fourth, 1854, Lincoln, at the same fair,
replied to Judge Douglas, contending that by the
Missouri Compromise, which covered the territory of Kansas and Nebraska, they had been
solemnly dedicated to freedom, and slavery pro-
hibited therein.

On October third, 1854, what was called an
Anti-Nebraska Convention was held at Springfield, at which twenty-six delegates were present, mostly well known Abolitionists. Lincoln
declined to attend this convention, as he was
not in sympathy with the doctrines of the Abolitionists. Moses, in his history of Illinois, says that
Lincoln met Douglas in joint debate in October,
1854, but does not state where, and that he
followed Douglas at Peoria and other places.[2]

Lincoln was elected to the Legislature from
Sangamon County in the fall of 1854. When
the returns of the election were made, and it was
shown that the opponents of the repeal of the
Missouri Compromise were in the ascendancy

[2]Lincoln and Douglas both spoke at Peoria on October
16. Lincoln made anti-Nebraska speeches at Urbana on
October 24, at Chicago on October 27, and at Quincy on
November 1. P.M.A.

28

in the General Assembly, as Lincoln was recognized as the leader in the Anti-Nebraska movement and the probable candidate for United States Senator to succeed Judge Breese,[3] he declined to accept his credentials as a member of the Legislature, and a special election was held to fill the vacancy.

When the General Assembly proceeded to the election of a United States senator, it was found that five of the Anti-Nebraska forces were old-time Democrats, and they refused to vote for Lincoln, who had always been a Whig. The result was that, in order to elect a senator who was opposed to the Kansas-Nebraska bill, Lincoln's friends, at his special instance, voted for Trumbull, who had always been a Democrat. The election of Trumbull to the Senate still left Lincoln the leader of the party in Illinois.

His correspondence with Judge Trumbull, lately published in a leading magazine, demonstrates that Lincoln kept his finger on the pulse of public sentiment and suggested the course to be pursued by the party in Illinois. In May, 1856, the first Illinois Republican State Convention was held in Bloomington. Lincoln was the

[3]James Shields, not Sidney Breese, was the Senator whom Lincoln sought to supplant. P.M.A.

central figure in that convention and made, what all who heard it pronounced, the greatest speech of his life. Most unfortunately, the speech was not reported and is now known as the "Lost Speech." I heard the speech and have read what purports to be the speech, as reproduced by Mr. Whitney, and must say that the reproduction does not strike me as being in any sense the speech which Lincoln made and which I heard.

I must hasten to speak briefly of the campaign of 1858. The Republican State Convention was held at Springfield, June 16, 1858, which nominated Lincoln for United States senator. It was at this convention that he made the speech containing the words above quoted: "A house divided against itself cannot stand," etc.

Moses, in history, says that when this speech was prepared it was submitted by Lincoln to his friends, and they all opposed that part of the speech. Lincoln said to them: "The time has come when these sentiments should be uttered, and if it is decreed that I should go down because of this speech, then let me go down linked to the truth—let me die in the advocacy of what is just and right."

In July, 1858, Douglas made his first speech in the campaign of 1858, at Chicago, from the balcony of the Tremont House, in which he vigorously attacked Lincoln's speech before the Republican Convention at Springfield in June. The next night Lincoln replied to Judge Douglas from the same place. July 16, 1858, Judge Douglas left Chicago for Springfield, and is reported to have spoken at Bloomington en route; and on July 17, 1858, he delivered a set speech at Springfield, to which Lincoln replied the next day. July 24, Lincoln challenged Douglas to joint debate, which a week later was accepted by Douglas and arrangements for the joint debates concluded.

The first debate occurred at Ottawa, August 21, 1858. At this time, Judge Douglas propounded seven questions to be answered by Lincoln at the next debate, to be held at Freeport. Before the Freeport meeting, Lincoln held a conference in Bloomington with his friends, at which he submitted his answers to Judge Douglas' questions. As to these there was no controversy. Then Lincoln announced to his friends that he proposed, at the Freeport meeting, to submit to Judge Douglas four questions, the principal one as follows: "Can the people in any territory, by any lawful means, against the wishes of any citizen of the United States, exclude Slavery from the territory, prior to its admission as a State?" Lincoln's friends, *except*

31

Jesse W. Fell, insisted that Judge Douglas would answer the question in a way that would certainly result in his election to the Senate and defeat Lincoln, to which Lincoln only replied that if he did so answer, he could never be president, and he, Lincoln, regarded the battle of 1860 for the presidency as infinitely more important than the senatorship.[4]

It should be remembered that before this time the Dred Scott decision had been rendered by the United States Supreme Court, which held that slave-holders had the right to take with them into any territory of the United States, their slaves, and hold them there so long as the territory remained a territory. Judge Douglas did reply as Lincoln's friends anticipated, that the Legislature of a Territory, by unfriendly legislation, might practically exclude slavery—that this was but carrying out his doctrine of popular sovereignty. Of course, this was in direct conflict with the Dred Scott decision, and this answer of Judge Douglas was spread broadcast over the South. The result was the secession of the South from the Democratic National Convention of

[4]Apparently Lincoln submitted his Freeport questions to many of his friends. Conferences like the one described by Judge Reeves have been reported from several towns and cities in northern Illinois, usually by someone who considered himself Lincoln's only confidant. P.M.A.

1860, and, in the end, the defeat of Judge Douglas for the presidency.

Judge Douglas, in the House of Representatives, and in the United States Senate, had established a national reputation as a debater. No man was better furnished with the weapons of debate, or exhibited more skill in their use, than he. On the other hand, Mr. Lincoln had only a State reputation, extending, perhaps, to some of the adjoining States, but no national reputation as a debater. In Illinois, Lincoln had the reputation of a logical debater. He had already measured swords with Judge Douglas, and each had received a taste of the other's metal. Doubtless, Judge Douglas' nation-wide reputation attracted marked attention to the debate the country over, and thereby Mr. Lincoln was brought into a national notoriety and prominence which later, in 1860, resulted in his nomination by the Republican party as its candidate for the presidency.

No sketch of Mr. Lincoln can be in any sense adequate which does not deal with his astonishing power over words. It is not too much to say of him, that he is among the greatest masters of prose ever produced by the English race. On this subject of Lincoln's power of expression, I will quote from a writer of the highest standing, a portrayal of the characteristics which gave to Lincoln his classic style of expression, that will, for all time, be the envy of those who strive for excellence in speech.

"The most striking characteristic of Lincoln's style may be found in the record from the beginning. Candor was a trait of the man and not less of his verbal manner. His natural honesty of character, his desire to make his meaning clear, literally to *demonstrate* what he believed to be the truth with mathematical precision—this gave to his expression both attractiveness and force. The simplicity of his nature, his lack of self-consciousness and vanity, tended to simplicity and directness of diction.

"An eminent lawyer has said—perhaps with exaggeration—that, without the massive reasoning of Webster or the resplendent rhetoric of Burke, Lincoln exceeded them both in his faculty of statement. His style was affected, too, by the personal traits of consideration of those of a contrary mind, his toleration and large human sympathy. But Lincoln's style might have had all these qualities and yet not have carried as it did. Beyond these traits comes the miracle—the cadence of his prose and its traits of pathos and of imagination. Lincoln's prose, at its height and when his spirit was stirred by aspiration and resolve, affects the soul like noble music. That is the strain in the two inaugurals, in the Gettysburg address, and in his letter of consolation to a bereaved mother, which moves the hearts of generation after generation.

"Lincoln's power of expression was evidently one

of the most effective elements of his leadership. The sympathy and toleration which made his writings and speeches so persuasive, assisted his leadership not only in convincing his listeners and in endearing him, the leader, to individuals and the masses, but helped him as a statesman to take large and humane views and to adopt measures in keeping with these views. To that sympathy and that toleration a reunited country is under constant obligation, not merely for the result of a successfully conducted war—successful in the true interests of both antagonists—but for the continuing possibility of good feeling between the sections. To think that in the preparatory political struggle and during the four years of the hideous conflict, Abraham Lincoln, though his spirit was strained almost beyond human endurance by the harassments of his position, though misunderstood and foully calumniated by public antagonists, and thwarted and plotted against by some of his own supporters, uttered not one word of violence or rancor—not a phrase which, after the cessation of hostilities, might return to embitter the defeated combatants or be resented by their descendants!"[5]

I will close this brief sketch with the closing sentence of the estimate of Mr. Lincoln by Mr. Herndon, his long-time law partner: "Take him all in all, he was one of the best, wisest, greatest and noblest of men in all the ages."

[5]Richard Watson Gilder, "Lincoln the Leader," in the *Century*, February, 1909. P.M.A.

Biographical Sketch of

HON. JAMES S. EWING

JAMES S. EWING *was born in 1835, in territory then a part of McLean County, but now included in Woodford County, Illinois. In 1840 his father, long a leading business man, removed to Bloomington and was at one time mayor of that city. Mr. Ewing prepared for college at a school called Jubilee College, situated in Peoria County. Later he graduated from Centre College at Danville, Kentucky. He read law at Bloomington and was admitted to practice in January, 1859, after which he spent a year in the office of Hon. John C. Bullitt, a leading attorney of Philadelphia, and, while in the latter city, he attended a course of law lectures. Since that time Mr. Ewing has practiced law at Bloomington, Illinois, with the exception of four years, during which time—1893-1897—he was United States Minister to Belgium. He has always been a Democrat, and always active in State and National politics, but was never a candidate for any political office. Mr. Ewing is still living at Bloomington, Illinois.*

Speech of
Hon. James S. Ewing

AT THE BANQUET OF THE ILLINOIS SCHOOLMASTERS'
CLUB, BLOOMINGTON, FEB. 12, 1909

Mr. Toastmaster and Gentlemen:

URING THE YEARS 1844 and 1845, my
father, Mr. John W. Ewing, was the proprietor
of the old National Hotel, on Front street, in the
city of Bloomington. At that time circuit courts
were held in McLean county, twice a year, and
there were a number of lawyers from other
counties who usually attended these terms.
Amongst those whom I specially remember as
coming from Springfield, and who were guests
at my father's house, were Hon. James
McDougall, afterward a Senator from California; Mr. John T. Stuart, and Abraham Lincoln. I thus became acquainted with Mr.
Lincoln, and I continued to know him, as a boy
knows a distinguished man whom he often

37

meets, until 1860, when he was elected President of the United States.

Mr. Lincoln was fond of children. At least he knew many of the boys and girls of the village, the children of his older friends, and often talked to them and expressed an interest in their welfare. They liked Mr. Lincoln, and most of the boys in the town knew him and many of them talked to him, as we all thought, on most intimate terms.

In 1844, Mr. Lincoln was thirty-five years of age, in the very prime of his younger manhood, and during the following fifteen years (except one term of service in Congress) he "traveled the circuit," devoting most of his time to the practice of the law. When I first knew anything of courts, Hon. Samuel H. Treat was the presiding judge of this circuit. He was afterward appointed to the Federal bench, and the Hon. David Davis became his successor and continued as the circuit judge until appointed by Mr. Lincoln as an associate justice of the Supreme Court of the United States. It was then the habit for such lawyers as possessed sufficient experience and ability to attract a clientage to follow the court around the circuit. Mr. Lincoln was of this number and more than perhaps any other was most constant and unremitting in his attendance.

During these fifteen years, with the eager curiosity of a boy, I was a frequent attendant in the court room, and heard Mr. Lincoln try a great many law suits. The suits themselves often dealt with trivial matters, but great men were engaged in them. Mr. Lincoln was engaged in most of the suits of any importance. He was wonderfully successful. He was a master in all that went to make up what was called a "jury lawyer." His wonderful power of clear and logical statement seemed the beginning and the end of the case. After his statement of the law and the facts in any particular case, we wondered either how the plaintiff came to bring such a suit or how the defendant could be such a fool as to defend it. By the time the jury was selected, each member of it felt that the great lawyer was his friend and was relying upon him as a juror to see that no injustice was done. Mr. Lincoln's ready, homely, but always pertinent, illustrations and anecdotes could not be resisted. Few men ever lived who knew, as he did, the mainsprings of action, secret motive, the passions, prejudices and inclinations which inspired the actions of men, and he played on the human heart as a master on an instrument.

This power over a jury was, however, the least of his claims to be entitled a good lawyer. He was masterful in a legal argument before the court. His knowledge of the general principles of the law was extensive and accurate, and his mind was so clear and logical that he seldom made a mistake in their application. Courteous to the court, fair to his opponent, and modest and restrained in his assertions, he was certainly the model lawyer.

As for myself, I decided I would be a lawyer, and that I would be just such a lawyer as Mr. Lincoln was. Well, as a matter of fact, I didn't become just such a lawyer. My failure in that regard, to my friends, was a regret rather than a surprise. I was like a rather frothy young friend of mine, who had been to hear Bishop Spaulding preach, and, inspired by the eloquence of the great preacher, imparted to me in confidence that "if he had his life to live over, he would be a bishop."

While my great ambition fell so far short of realization, yet of one thing I am sure—success was very much nearer by reason of the high ideals I imbibed from Lincoln. I believe that every young lawyer then at the Bloomington bar became a better lawyer on account of Mr. Lincoln's example.

I heard Mr. Lincoln make a number of political speeches. I heard his speech in the old court house in 1854, on the Kansas and Nebraska bill, in answer to the speech of Mr. Douglas on the same subject, made a few days before. In this speech, what impressed me most was that same wonderful power of statement to which I have before referred. I can never forget the manner in which he stated the causes and events which led up to the enactment of the Missouri Compromise; just what that compromise was, and how it affected the question of slavery; the history of the events and causes which led to the passage of the compromise of 1850; its constitutional elements; just what the South got and just what the North got by it, and how it was affected by the repeal of the other compromise bill. It seems to me I could almost repeat those statements to-day, after a half century, so vivid was the impression.

I heard his speech in the Major Hall Convention in May, 1856, spoken of sometimes as the "Lost Speech." But this speech did not impress me as the one of two years before—possibly because it was only one of several great speeches by other great orators—Owen Lovejoy, O. H. Browning, John M. Palmer, Archibald Williams, T. Lyle Dickey, Norton, Gridley, Farnsworth and others, who all took an active part in that historic convention.

In 1854, Judge Stephen A. Douglas came to Bloomington to make a speech defending the principles of the Kansas and Nebraska bill. Judge Lawrence Weldon, who was then a young lawyer at Clinton, and who had come up to hear the speech, went with Mr. Stevenson and myself to call upon and pay our respects to the "Little Giant." We were presented to Judge Douglas by Mr. Amzi McWilliams, then a prominent Democratic lawyer of this city. After we had been in Mr. Douglas' room a few minutes, Mr. Lincoln came in, and the Senator and he greeted each other most cordially as old friends, and then Mr. Douglas introduced Mr. Lincoln to Judge Weldon. He said: "Mr. Lincoln, I want to introduce you to Mr. Weldon, a young lawyer who has come to Illinois from Ohio, and has located at Clinton." Mr. Lincoln said: "Well, I am glad of that; I go to Clinton sometimes myself, and we will get acquainted." This was the beginning of an acquaintance which ripened into a strong friendship and which, founded on mutual admiration and respect, grew and strengthened as the years passed, and ended only in death. They met again at Clinton; a sort of local partnership was formed; they tried law suits and rode the circuit together. Judge Weldon was the active promoter of Mr. Lincoln's political interests, and was an

42

elector in the campaign of 1860. I doubt if any man living knew Mr. Lincoln better, or had in a greater degree his confidence, than our distinguished friend and citizen, Judge Lawrence Weldon.

In view of the recent controversy as to Mr. Lincoln's temperance principles, as to whether he was a "wine-bibber" or the "president of a temperance society," the following may be of interest: At this same meeting I heard Mr. Lincoln define his position on the liquor question. This is authentic, as coming from Mr. Lincoln himself, and ought to settle this question forever. But it won't. The controversy will go on, like the brook, "forever," until each side convinces itself. This meeting I am speaking of, being a Democratic meeting, the committee had placed on the sideboard of Judge Douglas' room (probably without his knowledge) a pitcher of water, some glasses and a decanter of red liquor. As visitors called they were invited to partake; most of the Democrats declined. When Mr. Lincoln rose to go, Mr. Douglas said, "Mr. Lincoln, won't you take something?" Mr. Lincoln said, "No, I think not." Mr. Douglas said, "What! are you a member of the Temperance Society?" "No," said Mr. Lincoln, "I am not a member of any temperance society; but I am temperate, *in this,* that I don't drink anything."

43

At the same meeting, another incident occurred which I wish to relate. One of the visitors who came to call on Senator Douglas was the Hon. Jesse W. Fell. He was an old friend, and had known Douglas when he first came to the State. I remember very well their cordial meeting and recall clearly a part of their conversation. After talking a while of old times and mutual friends, Mr. Fell said, "Judge Douglas, many of Mr. Lincoln's friends would be greatly pleased to hear a joint discussion between you and him on these new and important questions now interesting the people, and I will be glad if such a discussion can be arranged." Mr. Douglas seemed annoyed, and, after hesitating a moment, said: "No, I won't do it! I come to Chicago, and there I am met by an old line abolitionist; I come down to the center of the State, and I am met by an old line Whig; I go to the south end of the State, and I am met by an anti-administration Democrat. I can't hold the abolitionist responsible for what the Whig says; I can't hold the Whig responsible for what the abolitionist says, and I can't hold either responsible for what the Democrat says. It looks like dogging a man over the State. This is my meeting; the people have come to hear me, and I want to talk to them." Mr. Fell said: "Well, Judge, you may be right;

44

perhaps some other time it can be arranged."

I have told this incident for a purpose. Mr. Fell never gave up this idea of a joint discussion. He was the first man to suggest it. From 1854 to 1858 he continued to urge it, and to Mr. Jesse W. Fell, more than to any other man, is due the credit of bringing about those great debates, the full influence of which, upon Mr. Lincoln's fortunes, the events of history and the fate of the nation, no man is wise enough to know. Mr. Fell was the intimate, devoted, and *wise* friend of Mr. Lincoln. I speak with some knowledge and with perfect sincerity when I say that, with the possible exception of the Hon. David Davis, Mr. Fell did more than any other man, living or dead, to secure the nomination of Mr. Lincoln to the presidency.

Mr. Fell was one of our citizens. He was Bloomington's first lawyer. His life was a benefaction to this community. I am pleased to take advantage of this opportunity to connect his name with the name of the man he helped, and to pay a modest tribute to one of the best men that ever lived.

In the fall of 1860, I met Mr. Lincoln on the sidewalk in front of the old court house. He had come from Springfield to arrange some old suits, in view of his departure for Washington. He shook hands with me, and said: "Well, you have gotten to be a lawyer. Let me give you some advice: Don't meddle with politics; stick to the law." I replied: "Mr. President, I fear your example may prove more alluring than your advice." "No! no!" said he; "that was an accident." He passed into the court house, and that was the last time I ever saw him.[6]

Personal reminiscences must be confined to a time prior to 1860. The four years following belong to the history of the world.

This is the time of the making of many books, the writing of many histories, biographies, short and long sketches in magazines and newspapers, critiques and tributes, memoirs, stories, anecdotes and lies about Mr. Lincoln. There are books by His Private Secretary, by the "Man Who Knew Lincoln," by lots of men and women who didn't know him, by a member of the New York Bar, by members of other bars, by editors, schoolmasters and preachers, by "butlers, bakers and candlestick-makers," by "old neighbors" and

[6]This incident could not have taken place at Bloomington in the fall of 1860. Between May 18, 1860, when Lincoln was nominated for the Presidency, and February 11, 1861, when he started on his journey to Washington, he left Springfield only twice: the first time in November, 1860, for a trip to Chicago; and again, in January, 1861, to visit his step-mother in Coles County, Illinois. P.M.A.

46

by "old clients"—all about "Lincoln as a Boy,"
"Lincoln the Man," "Lincoln the Soldier," "Lincoln the Lawyer," "Lincoln the Story-Teller,"
"Lincoln the Lover," "Lincoln the Dreamer,"
"Lincoln the Farmer," the "Wood Chopper" and
the "Foot Racer." There will be delivered this
12th day of February, 1909, more than fifty
thousand speeches, addresses, orations and memorials which will help to swell this Lincolnian
literary melange to the proportions of an Alexandrian library.

It would be strange indeed, in view of the
many authors, the variety of publications and the
character of the subject, if there should not be
found an immense amount of misrepresentation,
false history, inaccurate estimates, false narrative,
tiresome repetitions, sentimental bathos, and silly
white lies. Old Doctor Johnson, when Boswell
told him he "intended to write his life," said, "If
I believed you, I would take yours." If Mr. Lincoln had been told what some of his friends
intended to do, he would have said with David,
"Oh, that mine enemy would write a book!"

The trouble is that men who never saw Mr.
Lincoln, and who have no adequate conception
of his life and character, have gotten up old
stories, incidents, traditions, second-hand anecdotes, and rushed into print to make history.

47

Others even manufacture goody-goody lies to increase his reputation. Others write of him as a slouch, a buffoon, an uneducated gawk, to increase the wonder of his career. Others tell of artful practices and doubtful tricks, to demonstrate his shrewdness. Others recite sentimental and impossible rescues and charities, which put old Santa Claus to shame. One old citizen tells of a wonderful conversation he had with Mr. Lincoln at the time of the Douglas and Lincoln debate at Bloomington—a debate which never took place. A reverend gentleman tells how an actor friend of his was invited by Mr. Lincoln to "stay all night" with him at the White House during the war; how they talked till midnight, and how Mr. Lincoln told him all the secrets of the war; how, when they had retired, the actor heard some one apparently in great distress; how he got up and wandered about the halls until he found Mr. Lincoln's private bedroom, and, looking through the keyhole, saw Mr. Lincoln on his knees, agonizing in prayer, etc. I suppose this preacher believed that proving Mr. Lincoln a saint justified him in proving his friend a liar and a sneak.

Another one of these stories is how Mr. Lincoln manufactured an almanac and introduced it in evidence to confound a witness who had sworn a certain night was moonlight, when the manufactured almanac showed it was the dark of the moon, thus saving his client's life. This story is repeated in Mr. Churchill's book, "The Crisis," and even in school books. No one who knew Mr. Lincoln can think of him as deliberately perpetrating a forgery upon the court, and practicing a trick of which only a pettifogger could conceive—a silly trick, too, which would certainly have been instantly exposed.

Another friend of Mr. Lincoln tells how he accompanied him to Washington from Springfield in 1860, and how the President "kept the entire company in constant roars of laughter" by telling questionable stories and jokes. It is probable this fellow was not on the train at all. I think there have been more lies told about Mr. Lincoln than about Santa Claus. A curious thing is that they are not usually malicious, but mostly told by mistaken friends and for good purposes. They are white lies, but I fear, unlike that of Uncle Toby and the loving lie of Desdemona, they will never be blotted out by the tears of the recording angel.

You and I can do little to stem this literary flood, but we can thank God that the subject of it is safe in the Pantheon, beyond the domain of human praise, blame or—stupidity.

Mr. Lincoln dressed as well as the average Western lawyer of his day. I do not think he gave much time to the tying of his necktie, and he could not have been said by his best friends to be much of a dude, but he was always respectably clothed. Mr. Lincoln was not a story-teller in the sense of "swapping stories," or telling a story for the sake of the story itself. He was possessed of great humor, and a wonderfully acute sense of the ridiculous. He had that marvelous "gift of the gods" which we sometimes call the "sixth sense." Unexpected situations, curious expressions, odd sayings, unusual appearances and humorous actions made an impression on him. He remembered these and often used them as illustrations. He seldom, if ever, told a story except to illustrate a point in his speech or argument, and in this kind of illustration no man was more apt. A few minutes after the voting in the legislature, in 1858,[7] when Mr. Douglas was elected Senator, Mr. Lincoln was asked by a friend, "How do you feel?" Said he, "I feel like the boy who stumped his toe: I am too big to cry and too badly hurt to laugh."

Hon. Ezra M. Prince, a Bloomington lawyer, who knew Lincoln very well, told the following story: After the adjournment of the Major Hall

[7]January 5, 1859. P.M.A.

convention, the Republican editors of Illinois met in convention at Bloomington. Mr. Lincoln attended and was invited to address the meeting.[8] He said he was afraid he was out of his place. He was not an editor, and had no business there; in fact, he was an interloper. He said: "I feel like I once did when I met a woman riding horseback in the woods. As I stopped to let her pass, she also stopped, and, looking at me intently, said, 'I do believe you are the ugliest man I ever saw.' Said I, 'Madam, you probably are right, but I can't help it!' 'No,' said she, 'you can't help it, but you might stay at home!'"

Hon. John B. Henderson, who was a Senator from Missouri during the war, told the following story, as showing how Mr. Lincoln could illustrate a situation by an incident: He said he was at the White House, talking with Mr. Lincoln. It was at a time when great pressure was being brought upon the President by certain radical members to induce him to issue an Emancipation Proclamation. Mr. Lincoln had been telling Mr. Henderson about his troubles in that regard. He did not think the time was ripe, and was very much annoyed at the per-

[8]The anti-Nebraska editors met at Decatur rather than Bloomington, and three months prior to the Bloomington convention instead of immediately after it. But Lincoln was in attendance, as Ewing stated. P.M.A.

sistence of three men whom he named—Senators Wade and Sumner, and Thaddeus Stevens, of Pennsylvania. All at once Mr. Lincoln said, "Henderson, did you ever attend an old field school?" "Yes," said the Senator. "Well," said Mr. Lincoln, "I did, and a funny thing occurred one day. You know, we had no reading books, and we read out of the Bible. The class would stand up in a row, the teacher in front of them, and read verses, turn about. This day we were reading about the Hebrew children. As none of us were very good readers, we were in the habit of counting ahead and each one practicing on his particular verse. Standing next to me was a red-headed, freckled-faced boy, who was the poorest reader in the class. It so fell out that the names of the Hebrew children appeared in his verse. He managed to work through Shadrach, fell down at Meshach, and went all to pieces at Abednego. The reading went on, and in due course of time came round again, but when the turn came near enough for the boy to see his verse, he pointed to it in great consternation, and whispered to me, 'Look! there come them three d——d fellers again.' And there," said Mr. Lincoln, pointing out of the window, "come those three same fellows." And sure enough, there were Wade, Stevens and Sumner, coming up the walk. Mr. Henderson added: "As I arose to take my departure, the other gentlemen entered, and there was a smile on Mr. Lincoln's face, as if his thoughts had flown away over all the years, from war and trouble, to the old field school in the forest of Indiana."

No one called Mr. Lincoln "Abe." Judge Davis, General Gridley, Mr. Isaac Funk, Mr. Fell, Leonard Swett, General William Ward Orme, Lawrence Weldon, William McCullough, Judge Treat, John T. Stuart, Owen T. Reeves, Reuben M. Benjamin, and William H. Hanna—all of them Lincoln's early friends and associates, and all of them elegant and dignified gentlemen—invariably addressed him as "Mr. Lincoln." It was always Mr. Clay, Mr. Webster, Mr. Lincoln.

It is a mistake to think of Mr. Lincoln as an ordinary man, even from the first. In 1844 he was a lawyer of state reputation; nine years before he was in the legislature, where he met such men as Douglas, McClernand, Browning, Ebenezer Peck, Robert Blackwell, Joseph Gillespie and Judge Purple. These were great men, and he was never dwarfed in their presence. I have spoken of the men with whom he associated and acted in our city. He was always easily the leader; he was the talker; everybody deferred to

Mr. Lincoln; he had the center of the stage by common consent. He knew more of the matter in hand. He thought more; he was a better talker, and was a natural leader.

When elected to the presidency, Lincoln did not select for his adviser, his private secretary and other unknown men, but William H. Seward, Edward Bates, Salmon P. Chase—all of whom had been prominent candidates in the Republican party for the presidential nomination, and to these were added other distinguished and leading men who constituted his Cabinet. He did not fear he would be overshadowed, and he never was. From the first he was the equal of any of them, and in Washington, as in Bloomington, he was the "Leader of Men."

It is a mistake to think of Mr. Lincoln as an uneducated man. The "kindergarten" and "primary" courses were taken in a Kentucky cabin, with his mother as "principal." Possibly he never learned at his school to make maps, but he did learn "manners and morals." At the age of nine he entered the academy to prepare for college. This "school of learning" was located in a "clearing" on his father's farm, a "little house in the woods" in the State of Indiana. Here his attention was first directed to "physical culture." This study he was not permitted to neglect. The "gymnasium" was well furnished with "apparatus"—axes, wedges, mauls, log-chains, cross-bars, swinging saplings, etc. Then came "nature study out on the campus." He found spring beauties and sweet williams, May-apples and purple grapes, and, out beyond, the prairie grasses and the wild rose. From these, from tree, shrub and plant, from form, color and perfume, came that sense of beauty embodied in those exquisite prose poems which we so much love to read. This branch of study included zoology. He learned the names of animals, their nature, habits, instincts, history and language. He knew when the birds mated and how they built their homes, and he learned well the lesson best worth learning from this science—to be kind and gentle to all animal nature.

He had lessons in political economy—the value of money; supply and demand; the virtue of economy; the proper sources of wealth; the lessons of necessity, and the value of labor. He closed his academic course at the age of twenty-one, with the honors of his class, and entered the university. He studied mathematics, became a surveyor and naval architect. He became a great linguist, and his success was all the greater in that he confined himself to one language. He devoted himself so diligently to the study of history that he learned how to make history.

He read and re-read Shakespeare, Burns and Byron. He studied some of the best English classics, and that wonderful volume of Hebrew literature, the Bible. The result of these "language studies" is the purest English ever written.

Rhetoric and logic came easy. He was a philosopher by nature. "Civil government" he learned under Jefferson, Madison and Hamilton. He took a post-graduate course in law under Professors Blackstone and Chitty, and from this department, as from the university and the academy, he carried away all honors, and was the valedictorian of his class. And yet there are pseudo historians and pretentious *litterati* who speak of Lincoln as illiterate and uneducated. I say, he was the best educated man in his day, if the best education means the best equipment for the duties of life.

There are a great many good Americans who are not exactly satisfied with Mr. Lincoln's ancestry. They can stand his poverty all right— that could be remedied—but a great man ought to have not only a father and a mother, but several grandfathers. In that marvelous transition from poverty to affluence, from a cabin to the White House, from obscurity to fame, the aching void is the want of ancestry. Mr. Lincoln, in his biography, gives the following account of his family:

"I was born February 12, 1809, in Hardin county, Kentucky. My parents were both from Virginia, of undistinguished families — second families, perhaps I should say. My mother, who died in my tenth year, was of a family of the name of Hanks, some of whom now reside in Adams county, and others in Macon county, Illinois. My paternal grandfather, Abraham Lincoln, emigrated from Rockingham county, Virginia, to Kentucky, about 1781 or 1782, where, a year or two later, he was killed by Indians, not in battle, but by stealth, when he was laboring to open a farm in the forest. His ancestors, who were Quakers, went to Virginia from Berks county, Pennsylvania. An effort to identify them with the New England family of the same name ended in nothing more definite than a similarity of Christian names in both families."

But this modest account, splendid in its simplicity, is by no means satisfying to the inquirer after a nobler lineage. Since we have known anything of the history of the human race, there has been traceable a disposition to make of the hero a demigod. Achilles, the son of Pelius, was also the son of Thetis. Alexander, after he had conquered the world, was the son of Hercules. Julius Cæsar became a descendant of Aeneas, who had a goddess for his mother. Moses no longer has a Hebrew mother, but is the son of the Pharaohs. This is only the symbolism of that disposition of human nature to account for great men and great achievements by greatness of birth.

But there is hope! I bring you good news! Mr. Lincoln's ancestors have been discovered! Two "distinguished genealogists," one an American and one an Englishman, have for years been collaborating to trace the ancestry of the great President to his English forebears, through colleges of heraldry and the records of the courts of chancery, for many generations. They have made many wonderful discoveries. The result of these genealogical labors is a book (I quote from the publishers) "which is a fine example of sound genealogical research, and is now offered at this centenary of Lincoln's birth," to a waiting public; "with elaborate tables, copious appendices, richly illustrated, and including "a defense of Thomas Lincoln, in one octavo volume, at ten dollars net"! [9] Mr. Lincoln had written it all in

[9] The reference is to J. Henry Lea and J. R. Hutchinson, *The Ancestry of Abraham Lincoln*, Houghton Mifflin, 1909. P.M.A.

58

twelve lines. These "distinguished genealogists require a quarto volume." Which do you like the better? Seriously, is it not strange, and is it not deplorable, that an intelligent American could believe that Saxon or Norman lineage could add anything to the fame of a man whose presence already fills the world? If his birth was lowly, his deeds are royal in that land which men call fame.

We are all hero-worshipers, and often, when our heroes are above the clouds, we build unto ourselves graven images. Sometimes their crowns are only tinsel, and are easily tarnished; sometimes their halos are only of paper and are very fragile. Men will differ as to the chief foundation of Mr. Lincoln's fame, but there will be no difference as to its being real and lasting. Some day, the true historian will appear. Some day, out of all this rubbish and jumble of inconsistencies, the true history will be written. Some day, when the rugged proportions of this great historic figure, by time and distance have been rounded into form, the real man will be known. Then, I think, we will come to realize that, in the history of a great man, chance is not so much a factor as Providence. Then we will understand better and appreciate more, how priceless was our heritage, and that, although given to the ages, "it was not taken from us."

Biographical Sketch of

COL. RICHARD PRICE MORGAN

RICHARD PRICE MORGAN *was born at Stockbridge, Massachusetts, on September 17, 1828, and died at Dwight, Illinois, May 20, 1910, which was after the address published in this book was delivered. In 1852, he came to Illinois in charge of the location and construction of what is now the Chicago & Alton Railroad, with his headquarters at Bloomington. Upon the completion of that road he became its general superintendent, in which capacity he served until 1857. He founded the city of Dwight, Illinois, and lived there with some interruptions until his death. In his later life he was connected with many very important engineering projects, and became a great authority in all engineering matters, serving at one time as chief engineer of the United States Pacific Railway Commission. In 1896 he was appointed by President Cleveland a member of the board of engineers to select a location and prepare plans and estimates for a deep water harbor on the southern coast of California. Later in life, the degree of Doctor of Engineering was conferred upon him by the University of Illinois.*

In 1860, when King Edward, then the Prince of Wales, visited the United States, Mr. Morgan entertained him, at Dwight, during his stay in that town on a hunt. Mr. Morgan was a large minded and public spirited man, and in his death, the State lost a most useful citizen. Of faultless dress and lofty and dignified bearing, "Col. Morgan" as he was called, was a typical gentleman of the old school.

Address of
Richard Price Morgan

AT PONTIAC, ILLINOIS, FEBRUARY 12, 1909,
ON "LINCOLN AT THE DECATUR CONVENTION"

Mr. President and Fellow
Citizens of Livingston County:

E HAVE ASSEMBLED to celebrate the coming of Abraham Lincoln, the mightiest human power and inspiration for good ever given to mankind. This is an auspicious day for this country and for the oppressed of all nations. It is being most earnestly celebrated throughout the world wherever Christianity has lifted up the people. In joining with you to celebrate this great period in the march of time, and in the history of our country, it is my duty to you as chairman of your delegation to the Republican State Convention at Decatur, Illinois, on the ninth and tenth of May, 1860, to give an accurate account to you of my stewardship.

Your delegation was selected at a county convention held in the old courthouse in Pontiac, early in May. The personnel of the delegation was: The late Hon. Jason W. Strevell, William Gagan, A. J. Cropsey, deceased, and Richard Price Morgan. It is fitting for me to say in this connection that Mr. Strevell, of Pontiac, was the first delegate chosen in the County Convention, and by priority and also by his fine abilities he naturally became chairman; but, on account of my acquaintance with and friendship for Mr. Lincoln, Mr. Strevell urged and, by his own motion, caused me to act as chairman of the delegation. I may appropriately add that your delegation worked in the convention in perfect harmony with the twelve delegates from McLean County, all of whom have passed away. Their enthusiasm for Lincoln was unbounded, and they claimed that the flint was first struck by Lincoln at Bloomington, that started the patriotic fires which lighted his way for the presidency.

My personal acquaintance with and friendship for Mr. Lincoln began in 1853, and continued until his death in 1865. The instructions we received when we were appointed delegates were to vote as a unit for State officers, and especially we were charged to do all in our power

63

to secure the passage of a resolution pledging the State of Illinois to the National Convention, about to assemble in Chicago, its patriotism and integrity, as represented in the person of Abraham Lincoln, to secure his nomination for the presidency.

Mr. Lincoln was personally present at the convention, and your delegates, as all others, had ample opportunity to meet and freely converse with him, upon the topics of the day. I shall not attempt to describe the intense patriotism which animated that most notable assembly. But to give you some idea of its spirit, I will repeat a short sentence from the speech of our War governor, Richard Yates, in acknowledging his nomination. He said: "Let us hope that the South will not attempt to destroy this Union; but, if it should, flaming giants will spring from every cornfield in the State of Illinois."

After the State business was concluded, the following resolution was unanimously adopted with unbounded enthusiasm. *Resolved*: "That Abraham Lincoln is the choice of the Republican party in Illinois for the presidency, and that the delegates from this State are instructed to use all honorable means to procure his nomination by the Chicago Convention, and that their vote be cast as a unit for him."

Mr. Lincoln was then escorted into the wigwam and to the platform by a committee selected by the chair. His appearance before the convention was the signal for another outburst of most hearty welcome. He received it without a smile, but the benignant expression of his eyes and face, and also his whole attitude, disclosed to every man in that multitude the affectionate gratitude of his heart.

The response of Mr. Lincoln to the resolution was in a few grateful words of thanks. At the close of his remarks, Livingston County first led off and gave the word—Three times Three for Abraham Lincoln, our next President. After these nine cheers were given with a will, the word came again from another part of the convention—Three times Three for Honest Old Abe, our next President. This was followed by another and another.

When quiet was partially restored, Mr. Lincoln came slowly down from the platform, shaking the hundreds of hands which were extended to him. At this juncture the rail committee, headed by Mr. Hanks, pressed through the crowd with several rails, carried them to the platform, and standing them up stood by them. Without further word the crowd, into which Lincoln had pressed his way some distance, commenced to shout "Identify your work." He was at once seized upon and carried in the arms and over the heads of the crowd to the platform again and placed beside the rails. Then the Convention, being again seated, shouted, "Identify your work! Identify your work!" After a moment's hesitation, addressing himself to the Convention, he said, quite solemnly, "I cannot say that I split these rails." Turning to Mr. Hanks and the committee, and looking at the rails, Mr. Lincoln asked: "Where did you get the rails?" Mr. Hanks replied: "At the farm you improved down on the Sangamon." "Well," said Lincoln, "that was a long time ago. However, it is possible I may have split these rails, but I cannot identify them." Again the Convention shouted, "Identify your work! Identify your work!" At this time the care visible on Mr. Lincoln's face gave way to a pleasant smile and he again said, "What kind of timber are they?" The committee replied, "Honey locust and black walnut." "Well," said Lincoln, his smile increasing, "that is lasting timber, and it may be that I split the rails." Then he seemed to examine the rails critically, his smile all the time increasing, until his contagious merriment was visible, and he laughingly said, "Well, boys, I can only say I have split a great many better looking ones."

This tactful turn was met by a storm of approval, and three times three were then given, and three more for "Honest Abraham Lincoln, the rail candidate, our next President."

The Convention then adjourned *sine die*. In a moment there was a rush of delegates to the platform. The rails were seized upon and pieces of some of them were sawed off for souvenirs. I am happy to say that Livingston County was again among the first to get two pieces, and that I have with me as a token of the rail episode of that convention parts of the pieces of rails brought home to Livingston County, now in the form of a gavel.

Nothing could have afforded more decisive proof that Lincoln did split the rails than his adroit presentation of the circumstantial evidence. This was at once recognized by every delegate and was received with delightful satisfaction. The significance of this rail episode in respect to the character of Mr. Lincoln and his subsequent conduct of the affairs of our country through its most dreadful trial, will be manifest to all thoughtful persons. His honesty, sagacity and tact were the foundations upon which he stood immovable, when saving our country, until the day of his death.

I have for this reason considered it my duty

in this respect especially to report to you and in the interest of accurate history state the facts which I have for so many years been possessed of in data and in an excellent memory. I feel so assured in what I have said that I do not believe it possible for any one to raise reasonable doubt of its general accuracy, nor shall I recede from any part of it without the indisputable proof of eye-witnesses like myself.

Soon after the adjournment of the convention, your delegation called on Mr. Lincoln to give him its best wishes and bid him good-bye for Livingston county. At that interview he said, in answer to a question as to his chances: "I reckon I'll get about a hundred votes at Chicago, and I have a notion that will be the high mark for me." This was the last duty of your delegation, and this report briefly represents the primary action of Livingston county in giving Abraham Lincoln to the world.

I have been requested to refer to some personal reminiscences of my relations with Mr. Lincoln. I had the good fortune to become acquainted with him in Bloomington in 1853, when I was division engineer, building the Chicago & Alton Railroad. Bloomington was then a village of 1,200 people, overcrowded with emigrants, land buyers, railway contractors and laborers. Being somewhat permanently located, I was fortunate enough to have a large room on the first floor of my boarding-house, to which circumstance I am indebted for my acquaintance with Mr. Lincoln. On a hot afternoon, I think in the autumn season, I was seated in my room with the door partly open to the main hall, when I overheard the following conversation: "Indeed, if you cannot accommodate me, I am sure I do not know what I shall do. I am here for this term of the Circuit Court, and have tried everywhere to find accommodations, but so far have failed, and I see no probability of success unless you can care for me." The landlady, to whom the above was addressed, replied: "Mr. Lincoln, I would like very much to give you a room and board while you are in the city, but I have no room or bed to offer you; but if it will help you any to come here for your meals, I will do the best I can for you." "Well," said Mr. Lincoln, "you are very kind, but I have nowhere to lay my head."

Those being early days of western life, of which I had seen something, I stepped to the hall door and for the first time saw the tall man of destiny. After a moment, I said to the landlady: "Is this gentleman a friend of yours?" To which she replied, introducing him as "Mr. Lincoln, of Springfield, a lawyer who is practicing

69

in the court of McLean county. He is a friend of mine, and I am very sorry indeed that I am unable to accommodate him." After looking at Mr. Lincoln a moment, and he at me, with a rather inquiring expression, I said: "If you will put a bed in my room, which is too large for one person in these crowded times, I would be pleased to have Mr. Lincoln room with me during his stay in the city." As I finished this remark, Lincoln threw back his head a little, and with it the long black hair that came over his forehead, and said: "Now, that is what I call clever."*

I thus became the roommate of the greatest man since Washington, the peer of any man in the love of liberty, justice and mercy; and I wish to record here that during the time of this stay—several weeks—I learned from him many things which have been of priceless value to me.

Although his time was very much engrossed by court proceedings, he seemed to strive, although I was twenty years his junior, to make his companionship interesting and serviceable to me. I was told by him of many things and stories of the earlier settlers in Illinois, and also he recited selections of poetry, one of them being

*In common western parlance the word "clever" was often used in the sense of *kind* or *accommodating*.

70

the poem, "Oh, why should the spirit of mortal be proud?" of which he was very fond.

One evening he said: "The people of McLean county, before they became interested in railway construction, and when Pekin, on the Illinois River, was their market, had very little to occupy their time, especially at some seasons of the year. They would come to Bloomington on Saturdays with all sorts of vehicles—wagons, carts, and on horseback—and put in most of the day in fun, horse racing, settling old feuds, etc. When evening came and they were about to separate and return to their homes, almost every man, besides being well filled before starting, carried with him a good-sized brown jug in the front end of his wagon or cart."

Speaking of the relative merits of New England rum and corn juice, as he called it, to illuminate the human mind, he told me this story of John Moore, who resided south of Blooming Grove, and subsequently became State Treasurer: Mr. Moore came to Bloomington one Saturday in a cart drawn by a fine pair of young red steers. For some reason he was a little late starting home, and besides his brown jug, he otherwise had a good load on. In passing through the grove that night, one wheel of his cart struck a stump or root and threw the pole out of the ring of the yoke. The steers, finding themselves free, ran away, and left John Moore sound asleep in his cart, where he remained all night. Early in the morning he roused himself, and looking over the side of the cart and around in the woods, he said: "If my name is John Moore, I've lost a pair of steers; if my name ain't John Moore, I've found a cart." After a good laugh together, Lincoln said: "Morgan, if you ever tell this story, you must add that Moore told it on himself."

On the adjournment of the Circuit Court, Mr. Lincoln returned to Springfield, after which I only met him incidentally when visiting Springfield, until the following autumn, when I became superintendent of the Chicago & Alton Railway, soon after which I engaged the services of Mr. Lincoln as attorney and counselor for the company, and thereafter had frequent business intercourse with him.

It is not necessary for me to speak of his then acknowledged ability at the bar, but to illustrate his touch of humor and knowledge of human nature, which was ever present with him, I quote a letter which I received from him, inclosing an expired annual pass for 1855, and requesting its renewal, which was due him as counsel for the company:

"Springfield, Feb. 13, 1856.—R. P. MORGAN, ESQ.:
Says Tom to John, 'Here's your old rotten wheelbar-
row. I've broke it usin' on it. I wish you would mend
it, 'case I shall want to borrow it this arternoon.' Acting
on this as a precedent, I say, 'Here's your old 'chalked
hat.' I wish you would take it and send me a new one,
'case I shall want to use it by the 1st of March.'
"Yours truly, A. LINCOLN."

I have always understood that this letter was
written to me more as an acquaintance and
friend than in my official capacity. The expression "chalked hat" was at that era, in railroad-
ing, at least, quite generally used in connection
with persons who were fortunate enough to
possess annual passes, and when they were called
upon by the conductors, the holders would say,
"I have a chalked hat," or, in brief, "I chalk."

It was in the summer of the year that I received this letter—1856—that I stood next to Mr.
Lincoln and heard him say: "You can fool some
of the people all of the time, and all of the people some of the time, but you can't fool all of the
people all of the time." He was addressing an
assemblage of about three or four hundred people from the raised platform of the entrance
to the Pike House, in Bloomington, Ill., upon
the subject of the Kansas-Nebraska Act, and re-
viewing the arguments of Douglas in support

of it. His application of his epigram was so apt and so forcible that I have never forgotten it, and I believe that no verbal modification of it would be accurate.[10] In his final peroration of that address, referring again to the arguments favoring the Kansas-Nebraska Act, he said, with wonderful energy and earnestness: "Surely, surely, my friends, you cannot be deceived by such sophistries."

The occurrences of which I have spoken were all anterior to the war to preserve the Union. Among some treasures I have is an autograph letter, written in 1863, in which Mr. Lincoln declares himself to be my personal acquaintance and friend.

I consider it my duty to mention one fact that may otherwise be lost in the history of our county, as seemingly there is no record of it. Upon the call of President Lincoln for 75,000 volunteers, "Flaming Giants" did spring from the cornfields of Livingston county. On the 16th of April, the morning after the call, at 5 o'clock, I had the honor of standing at the door of the Adjutant General's office in the old State House

[10]This apothegm, so confidently attributed to Lincoln, is nowhere to be found in his published writings or speeches. In 1905 several men claimed that he used it at Clinton, Illinois, in 1858. See Nicolay and Hay, *Complete Works of Abraham Lincoln*, New York, 1905, III, 349n. P.M.A.

at Springfield, holding in my hand a muster roll of eighty volunteers from Livingston county. It was recorded as No. 13, twelve others only standing ahead of me in the line, and before the office opened there were as many behind me, holding up their muster rolls. These volunteers from Livingston county were not mustered in as a company, because there were more volunteers in the State at large than its quota under that call. Most of these men immediately sought service in Regiments Seven to Twelve, inclusive, which constituted the First Brigade of Illinois Volunteers, organized from April 25 to May 10, 1861.

Biographical Sketch of

JUDGE FRANKLIN BLADES

JUDGE FRANKLIN BLADES *was born November
29, 1830, in Rush County, Indiana. He was the
son of a country physician, but lost his father
at the age of sixteen. In his youth, there were
few schools in Indiana, and none free. He
therefore got in youth only such education as
he could pick up at home and under private tu-
tors. He was, however, fortunate enough to ac-
quire in his youth a love for good books, and
in time he became a man of cultivated mind
through the study of such authors as Irving,
Goldsmith, Johnson, Shakespeare, Addison and
others. In 1852 he graduated from the Rush
Medical College of Chicago, and subsequently
took post-graduate courses in medicine in the
University of Pennsylvania and in Jefferson
Medical College at Philadelphia. He early settled down to his life work at Watseka, Illinois.
He was the editor of a Republican newspaper,
supporting Fremont for the presidency in 1856.
In the latter year he was also elected to the Illinois Legislature. Again, in 1860, he was elected
and served in the legislature.*

In 1858, having studied law in the meantime, he was admitted to the Illinois bar. Subsequently, in 1862, he reverted to his original profession of medicine long enough to serve as surgeon of the 76th Illinois Infantry. In 1864 he was a Republican presidential elector for Illinois, and had the satisfaction of voting for his friend, Abraham Lincoln, for his second term. In 1877 Blades was elected to the circuit bench for a short term, and in June, 1879, he was re-elected for a full term of six years. In January, 1888, because of ill health, he removed to California, and is now living and raising oranges at Pomona in that State. A short biography of himself which the Judge prepared for the publishers of this book, closes with these modest words:

"And now as I near the close of my long life I recall with affection, and almost tearful gratitude, the memory of the many friends whose kindly offices did so much to promote such success as I have had, and which I think quite equal to my merits."

Recollections of
Judge Franklin Blades

HAD SOME PERSONAL ACQUAINTANCE
with Mr. Lincoln. The first time I met him was
in a caucus of the Republican members of the
Illinois House of Representatives, of which I
was a member, in the winter of 1857. The meeting was held in Mr. Lincoln's office in Springfield, Illinois. I was much interested in observing
his homely, friendly, cordial manners, and the
candor and good sense in what he had to say.
There were those of the Senate and House who
had been elected in opposition to Democratic
candidates, but who had not become identified
with the new Republican party. These men not
long afterward became Republicans. Among
these was Senator Gillespie, subsequently gen-

erally known as Judge Gillespie. He had been an old Whig friend of Mr. Lincoln. During the session of our caucus, Mr. Lincoln said: "Boys, what do you say to having old Joe Gillespie in here?" There being general assent, the Senator was sent for, and it was interesting to see the cordial, friendly manner in which they greeted each other. I afterward came to know Judge Gillespie quite well, and have heard him say many an affectionate word concerning his old friend, years after that old friend had, by the universal acclaim of mankind, been enshrined among the immortals.

I once attended a reception by Mr. and Mrs. Lincoln at their old-fashioned residence in Springfield. The invitation I received was in the handwriting of Mr. Lincoln. I have it yet. The guests were received in an informal and friendly manner by Mrs. Lincoln. On being ushered upstairs I found Mr. Lincoln and the Democratic State Auditor, whose name, as I remember it, was Jones,[11] sitting on a high post bed, chatting with each other, Mr. Lincoln particularly greeting all who came into the room. Mr. Lincoln was not then talked of for the presidency—certainly not outside of his own State.

[11]A bad guess. No Illinois State Auditor in Lincoln's lifetime bore the name Jones. P.M.A.

In the spring of 1858, having been admitted to the bar, and intending to give up the profession of medicine, I wrote to Mr. Lincoln, requesting the use of his name as a reference on my professional card as a lawyer. He had known me as a physician, and in writing to him I said nothing about my change of profession, and so in replying he seemed to be in doubt as to whether I was the same Blades he had known. So he wrote: "I do not know whether you are Dr. Blades or not. If you are Dr. Blades, you may use my name; if you are not Dr. Blades, if Dr. Blades says you may use my name, you may do so."

Some time afterward I met him in Springfield, and taking me by the hand he said, with an amused twinkle in his eye: "You got my letter, did you?" And then he repeated it. The excuse I offer for introducing this incident, so personal to myself, is its quaintness of style, so characteristic of him, and so graphically apparent in the famous and caustic reply to Mr. Greeley. I don't know what became of the letter, but I think that it was stolen from among my papers when packing for my move to California.

I was a member of the Republican State convention of 1858, before which Lincoln made the famous speech in which he repeated the saying of Christ, that a house divided against itself cannot stand, and in which he contended that the States of the Union must all become free or all slave. He gave no hint that he was in favor of division, or that he was in favor of the domestic institutions of all the States becoming the same; but Stephen A. Douglas, in campaigning over the State, seeking re-election as Senator, perverted and misstated and misrepresented what he said, and contended that Mr. Lincoln was really in favor of making the domestic institutions the same in all the States. Mr. Lincoln had said that he did not believe that the Union would be dissolved, but did believe that the opponents of slavery would arrest the further spread of it, and place it where the public mind would rest in the belief that it was in the course of ultimate extinction; or its advocates "would push it forward, till it would become alike lawful in all the States, old as well as new, North as well as South." His manner of delivery of that speech was calm, deliberate, dispassionate and without a single gesture. There were over-cautious Republicans who thought that he had better have omitted some things that he said; and, in fact, it formed the principal capital stock of Mr. Douglas in his campaign for the senatorship; but the result demonstrated that Lincoln was a great political prophet and statesman.

I was a delegate to the State Republican convention which met at Decatur, the county seat of Macon county, in 1860, which selected the delegates to the National Convention, then soon to meet in Chicago for the purpose of nominating a candidate for the presidency, and which instructed those delegates to support Mr. Lincoln's candidacy. Mr. Lincoln was present and was seated on the platform during the session of the convention. While the convention was in session, Mr. Hanks, a cousin of Mr. Lincoln, and another man came into the hall, bearing aloft two old rails, between which was stretched a banner on which was printed the statement that the rails were a part of a lot of rails made by Mr. Lincoln in the county of Macon, many years before. Mr. Hanks had at the time worked with Mr. Lincoln in making the rails, and personally no doubt remembered better than Mr. Lincoln could then recall that the statement was true. When the rails were brought in, the entire body of the delegates rose to their feet, waving their hats and cheering at the top of their voices, and shouting, "Lincoln! Lincoln! Lincoln!" He came to the front of the platform looking very much amused, holding his hands folded in front of him. He spoke briefly, saying it was true that when he was a young man he made some rails in Macon county, but he really could not say whether the rails brought in by Mr. Hanks were a part of the lot or not. I have seen a statement in some magazine that this incident occurred in the National Convention at Chicago, but I personally know that it did not, for I was present in both conventions, though not a delegate in the Chicago convention. Of course, it would not have been tolerated in the National Convention, where there was more than one candidate for the nomination.

I do not think that Mr. Lincoln was very confident of being nominated at Chicago. A friend and neighbor of his from Springfield said that before coming away he inquired of him if he was going to attend the convention. Mr. Lincoln replied that he was not; that he was most too much of a candidate to attend, and hardly enough of a candidate to stay away.

I was considerably younger than Mr. Lincoln and, besides, did not see him frequently enough to become on terms of intimacy with him. He knew enough of me to regard me as a personal and political friend, and I knew enough of him to know that many of the purported anecdotes that I have often read of him were gross and scandalous caricatures of him. He was hearty and cordial in manner toward those with whom he was on terms of friendship. I was particularly indignant when I read the coarse and vulgar fiction of him which appeared in "The Crisis." The vulgar, ill-bred familiarity which, in "The Crisis," characterizes the supposed intercourse between Mr. Lincoln and Mr. Joseph Medill is repulsive and without the least foundation in the character of either of them. Medill was considerably younger than Mr. Lincoln, and had no intimate or long-standing acquaintance with him. While Mr. Lincoln was not in the least assertive of his dignity and self-respect, yet there was that about him which would prevent any one from slapping him on the back and calling him "Abe," except it might possibly be the few who were familiar with him from his young manhood and who had kept pace with him in his gradually increasing social standing.

In the long past I occasionally heard interesting and amusing anecdotes of Mr. Lincoln by Judge Weldon and others who used to meet him at the bar of the old eighth judicial circuit, in which Judge David Davis presided, but I cannot recall them with sufficient distinctness to make it worth while to relate them. It is true

84

I might supply the want of memory by fictions, as some of his biographers have done.

An anecdote told me many years ago by my friend Beckwith, a lawyer of Danville, Illinois, now lamented as dead, I will venture to relate. Mr. Lincoln and Mr. Vorhees, a distinguished lawyer, a sometime United States Senator for Indiana, were engaged on opposite sides of a suit in the Circuit Court of Danville. In arguing a question to the judge, Mr. Vorhees made some discourteous and rather offensive remarks about Mr. Lincoln. When Mr. Lincoln came to reply he so unmercifully and at the same time so humorously ridiculed Mr. Vorhees that some of the lawyers ran out of the court house and lay down on the grass in explosions of laughter. Mr. Vorhees took great offense, and in the evening called at the room where Mr. Lincoln, Judge Davis and some others were engaged in social chat, and furiously assailed—not assaulted —Mr. Lincoln, but he came off much worsted, as he had in the discussion before the judge.

It is much to be lamented that Judge David Davis did not leave on record his recollections of Mr. Lincoln. Mr. Lincoln practiced many years before him, and they were probably on more intimate terms than any others after Mr. Lincoln began the practice of the law. Judge Davis was a man of infinite humor, which often cropped out while on the bench, and could heartily appreciate the humor of Mr. Lincoln. Why did he not leave memoirs of his intimate friend, to be read through all time?

In 1861 I was a member of the Illinois House of Representatives, elected as a Republican, and was present during the entire regular session, beginning in January, and also attended the special session convened in April, on the calling for 75,000 troops by the President on the fall of Fort Sumter. That winter, during the sitting of the regular session, was the most gloomy and despondent period of my life. I felt sure that the Southern States meant permanent secession even if they had to fight for it. But they did not anticipate civil war. In the South it was generally believed that the people of the North were so commercialized and were so divided in partisanship that war for the Union would be "impossible." On the other hand, the levity with which the secession movement was for the most part regarded by Republicans, and which was distinctly manifest among the Republican members of the legislature, to me was inexplicable and depressing. Sensible men, and even good friends, regarded my gloomy apprehension as next thing to absurd.

During the session of the legislature, a convention of the Democracy was held in the hall which had been given up to them by vote of the House. I was a lobby onlooker of that convention, and the incendiary speeches which were made and applauded to the echo, and the misapprehensions of Mr. Lincoln, were so vividly impressed on my memory that now, nearly fifty years after, they are recalled with almost startling distinctness. Among my papers I have preserved a copy of the *Missouri Republican* (now the *Missouri Republic*), of the date of January 19, 1861, purporting to give a *verbatim* report of the speeches. Among the most eloquent was that of Henry S. Fitch, Buchanan's United States District Attorney for the Northern District of Illinois. The speech itself was not disloyal, but the responses it drew out showed the temper of the members to be as favorable to the South as the most fiery secessionist could wish. Fitch played on that convention as if it were a musical instrument. Among other things, he said: "This Union was purchased by blood; it was cemented by blood; and isn't it worth saving by blood now?" "No, No!" was the universal response. "I say it is," said he, and that was hissed. And then he said, "But blood won't save it," and that was uproariously applauded. The report in the paper states that when he said it was worth saving by blood he was greatly applauded, but that applause came from Republicans who had gathered in the lobby. Poor, dear, loyal, brilliantly eloquent fellow! he died in the far South, a major in the Union army.

A Mr. William Homes made a speech. Among other things, he said:

"Gentlemen of the Convention and Fellow Citizens: I know one thing to be true: that it would be no difficult matter to produce civil war in Illinois. I know that the state of feeling which might be fanned into a flame is so deep here in this city now that, if it correctly represents, as I believe it does, the feelings of the State, it might break out into an act of secession at home, and Illinois thus become a divided State."

R. T. Merrick, of Chicago, among many other things, said:

"I feel that I cannot be in error when I say that this Union *never can be saved by force.* Coercion! — force! This is war — war upon the Southern States—not on South Carolina alone —not on the cotton States alone—but upon the *entire South.* For be assured, gentlemen, that whether the border States follow the secession of States of the extreme South or not, they will most certainly regard any hostile attack upon these Southern States as an attack upon themselves. It will be a war, then, upon fifteen States. Are you prepared for such a war? (Shouts of *'No, no! Fight here!'*) No, gentlemen, thank God! fanaticism has not yet so hardened our hearts that we are ready to imbrue our hands in the blood of our brothers. (Applause.) Such a war would be most accursed, wicked, unjust, cruel and diabolical; and if the Republican leaders expect that it would be a war in the Southern States—a war at a distance so far removed from the North that those who had brought it on would not even be disturbed by the roar of its cannon, let them undeceive themselves at once. The tone and feeling of this convention responds to my own; and I am satisfied that, if such a conflict ever comes, it will be war *in the North, and not war in the South.* (Applause.) It will be war in Chicago—war in Springfield—war on the broad prairies of Illinois. (Loud applause.) Before the patriotic people of this State will allow an invading force to pass beyond its borders to subjugate the South, they will make one vast mausoleum of your State. (Continued applause.)"

89

Mr. Richardson, not long before a Senator of the United States, in his speech to the convention, said: "Why, Mr. Lincoln has said, and Mr. Seward has said, 'Away with this doctrine of the inequality of races. It is in violation of the Declaration of Independence. The government cannot endure half slave and half free.' Mr. Seward said in Ohio: 'You, my friends, must turn in and help me; we can extinguish this thing of slavery.'" How false he must have known his words to be!

Now, at the time this convention was being held, the South Carolina legislature was pushing through a bill to call out and arm 10,000 troops; and batteries were being erected to bombard Fort Sumter. Four States had already seceded. Senators and representatives from these States were resigning from the House and Senate. And yet, if this threatened war on the part of the South were resisted, we were told there would be war in Illinois—war in Chicago. No word of sympathy for Mr. Lincoln, who, in his home, not much more than a stone's throw from the hall of the convention, was brooding sadly, weighed down with the awful responsibility that rested on him to save the Union, if, in the face of a united South, and the great body of an intensely hostile party in the North, it could be saved. Everything was said calculated to encourage the secessionists. Mr. Lincoln and the man he had determined on to be his Secretary of State were misrepresented as holding sentiments hostile to the South, which they had never expressed, and did not entertain. I relate these things here to show the situation—the awfully discouraging situation—that Mr. Lincoln faced in January, 1861.

Governor Yates was condemned for recommending a reorganization of the militia. In the House a Democrat (Green of Massac) moved to amend the militia bill by providing that the militia be armed with cornstalks; and yet these people professed to be in favor of the Union. Yes; but it was to be only such a Union as would be satisfactory to the most radical of the slaveholders. But even that sort of a Union these slaveholders would not then have accepted. They disliked the Northern *people*. They were more unlike the Northern people than they were unlike the people of England. Their manners were different from ours. Their education had been different. Their dialect was different. Slavery had made them aristocrats. They placed the laboring man on a level with their negroes. They expected to win without civil war. And they would have won had they not fired a gun—if they had not attacked Fort Sumter.

The Springfield convention, in response to Democratic conventions which had been held in Kentucky and Indiana, as a means of conciliating the South, recommended the calling of a convention of all the States to amend the constitution. The *Missouri Republican,* in an editorial discussing this method of settling the trouble, recommended that *resort to secession* as a remedy should be had only after "all other means of reconciliation have been exhausted."

In the midst of the gloom and portents of the on-coming tragedy of civil war, Mr. Lincoln showed a willingness to conciliate the great Northern party which was so thoughtlessly feeding the fires of secession. He was willing to concede something in the way of compromise which did not contemplate a surrender of the principles of which he had been the foremost advocate, and which he deemed not to be inconsistent with the domestic institutions of the slaveholding States; for he was naturally a conservative man, and always held that by virtue of the constitution the slaveholder was entitled to have his fugitive slaves returned to him. No compromise could be framed that would stop the agitation by those in the North who believed that slavery was sinful. He, with the great majority of the North, believed slavery to be wrong, but they faithfully regarded the constitutional obligation to protect it in the slaveholding States. Nor could any compromise prevent the operations of the underground railroad, which but few, comparatively, were engaged in conducting, but in the operation of which everybody would have taken part if secession had succeeded.

Deeming it not unwise to make some response to the sentiment which seemed to be so extensively entertained, not only in Illinois, but throughout the North, in favor of offering compromise, as expressed by the Illinois convention, even if no other effect should be produced than to demonstrate the folly of expecting that the South would entertain any proposition of compromise whatever, Mr. Lincoln drafted a preamble and resolutions which he caused to be adopted by the Illinois legislature, which were entered in the House and Senate journals, as follows:

"Mr. Jarrot, from the Committee on Federal Relations, to which was referred sundry resolutions referring to the condition of the Union, reported the same back with the following preamble and resolutions:

"WHEREAS, Although the people of the State of Illinois do not desire any change in our Federal Constitution, yet as several of our sister States have indi-

93

cated that they deem it necessary that some amendment should be made thereto; and

"WHEREAS, In and by the Fifth Article of the Constitution of the United States, provision is made for proposing amendments to that instrument, either by Congress or by a convention; and

"WHEREAS, A desire has been expressed in various parts of the United States for a convention to propose amendments to the Constitution; therefore, be it

"*Resolved by the General Assembly of the State of Illinois,* That if application shall be made to Congress by any of the States deeming themselves aggrieved, to call a convention, in accordance with the constitutional provision aforesaid, to propose amendments to the Constitution of these United States, that the Legislature of the State of Illinois will and does hereby concur in making such application.

"*Resolved,* That until the people of these United States shall otherwise direct, the present Federal Union must be preserved as it is, and the present Constitution and laws must be administered as they are; and to this end, in conformity to that Constitution and the laws, the whole resources of the State of Illinois are hereby pledged to the Federal authorities.

"*Resolved,* That copies of the above preamble and resolutions be sent to each of the Representatives and Senators in Congress and to the Executives of the several States."*

*The preamble and resolutions were voted on separately and as a whole and adopted by the House. (House Journal, pp. 301, 302, 303, 304, Feb. 1.) Concurred in by Senate. (Senate Journal, p. 231, Feb. 2, 1861.) Concurrence reported back to House. (House Journal, p. 534, Feb. 13, 1861.) Printed also in the public laws of 1861, p. 281.

This important document has so far escaped the historian, for at the time of its passage it did not purport to come from Lincoln. There is no record that he had anything to do with it; nor was it publicly given out that he wrote the resolutions. But I know very well that he did write them. It was not concealed from the Republican members of the Legislature that he wrote them. I was very well acquainted with every Republican member, and I know that no one of them claimed to be the author. I do not remember who introduced them, nor, indeed, that anyone did. I have the impression, though indistinct after the lapse of nearly fifty years, that no one did, but that they were privately handed to Mr. Vital Jarrot, chairman of the Committee on Federal Relations, and by him reported to the House. I sat near Mr. Jarrot during the entire session and was on familiar, almost intimate, terms with him. I think it was from him that I received my impression as to the authorship.[12] Mr. Jarrot was a most excellent, sensible gentleman and a true patriot. He was one of the not many Republican members of the House who deemed it important that some offer of compromise should be made,

[12]The reader should note well the tenuous evidence on which Judge Blades attributed these resolutions to Lincoln. P.M.A.

95

though having but little faith that any offer would be accepted by the Southern people. He thought that it should be offered for its effect on our political opponents, if no other benefit should come of it.

It failed to effect anything, and it remained for the firing on Sumter to disabuse the minds of those who professed to be hopeful that the South would yield to compromise. The many thousands of Southern Illinois, relied on by the Springfield orators to fight in Springfield and in the streets of Chicago, led by the brilliant and gallant Logan, rallied under the banner of the Union on the bloody fields of the South.

I heard the last speech Senator Douglas ever made. On the invitation of the House of Representatives of Illinois, at the special session in April, 1861, he made a strong and patriotic appeal for a united effort in resisting the attempt of the slave power to destroy the Union. His towering ambition to become President (from the much lower moral plane on the subject of slavery than that of Mr. Lincoln) had tumbled to ruin. I have a vivid recollection of the appeal he made on the one hand to the Republicans to use with moderation, and in a spirit of conciliation to their Democratic opponents, the control they had come to have in the affairs of the government;

and on the other hand, to his Democratic friends, "not to allow their opposition to the Republican party to turn them into traitors to their country." This almost startling expression aroused angry feeling in many Democratic members, and it was suppressed in the printed speech, but I was sitting near him and I know he said it. Poor man! From Springfield he went home to Chicago, soon to die in the full prime of his great powers, for he was only forty-eight years of age. Often, often since I have thought of the solemn words, "Death, death, death," he uttered as he lay on his deathbed in the old Tremont House in Chicago. Had he not died he might have greatly distinguished himself on the fields of war, and finally become President of the United States.

People of a later generation can have no adequate appreciation of the intense hostility, and even hatred, with which Mr. Lincoln was regarded by his political opponents. We who lived then and were heartily with him in his efforts to maintain the Union could see, and did see, that many of them exulted when they heard that he was killed. They dared not much to show it, else they themselves would have been killed. Blinded by intense partisan spirit, and blind to the fact that the slave power had long been planning either to make it lawful to carry their slaves into every quarter of the Union or to dissolve the Union, they laid the whole trouble at the door of those who were simply resisting the further extension of slavery.

The principal organ of these opponents of Mr. Lincoln in Illinois was the *Chicago Daily Times,* owned and edited by Wilbur F. Storey. On the first day of July, 1864, it published an editorial out of which I cut the following extract:

"We have no disposition to taunt Kentucky in her present condition, but if this resolution is true (referring to a resolution of the Democratic State Convention held on the 28th of June) we must infer that her people are not free. Democratic newspapers are not permitted to circulate in the State, and she is deprived of the other enumerated essentials of a free government. She is not thus bound because her sons are 'pigeon-livered and lack gall to make oppression bitter,' but she waits and hopes that she may be unfettered without resorting to force to re-establish law. She will not wait many months, nor will the nation delay in rising to her rescue if a fraudulent presidential election should in form re-invest Mr. Lincoln in his present office. He cannot be fairly and lawfully elected, and the people have determined that he shall not hold office if elected by fraud. He could not be more worthless dead than he is living, but he would be infinitely less mischievous, and his corpse, repulsive as it would be in its freshest state and richest and most graceful habiliments, would yet be the most appropriate sacrifice which the insulted nation could offer in atonement for its submission to his imbecility and despotism."

Who could doubt that that man Storey and the patrons of his paper rejoiced in their secret souls when their tool, John Wilkes Booth, shot Lincoln down on the night of April 14, 1865? When General Burnside was in command of the department of Ohio, he ordered the *Chicago Times* to be suppressed. Mr. Lincoln's "despotism" was such that he countermanded the order!

Recollections
of Abraham Lincoln

BY MR. JOHN W. BUNN
OF SPRINGFIELD, ILLINOIS, RELATED IN A
CORRESPONDENCE WITH ISAAC N. PHILLIPS

LETTER OF MR. PHILLIPS

Bloomington, Illinois, October 25, 1910

Mr. John W. Bunn, Springfield, Ill.

MY DEAR SIR: You have often, in idle hours, related to me your recollections of Lincoln. I feel that some of the things you have told me should be preserved in a permanent form. I am just now helping to get out a little book of recollections of Lincoln by a number of men who knew him quite well. I am sure no man now living had a nearer view of Lincoln, in the period covered by the last dozen years before his assumption of the presidency, than you had. I am further sure that no man's recollections of Lincoln at that period are clearer or more reliable than yours. You are not a man who is disposed to state doubtful things or to try to exaggerate your own knowledge of, or associations with, Mr. Lincoln. Others have been less modest.

Very few men are now living who knew Lincoln well before the war—certainly but few whose recollections are to be depended upon. I am persuaded that much is now related concerning Lincoln that is of very doubtful authenticity. I therefore feel I have some right to ask you to put in form some of the things you have often told me in private conversation. I wish you to state what kind of a man Lincoln was socially, and what kind of a man he was as a politician, if he was a politician. Please embody these recollections and estimates in a letter to me, so I may preserve them in a permanent form and give them publicity. Some errors which have crept into the public mind may thus be corrected, and you will have helped to give the future a more correct view of the most interesting if not the greatest, character of modern times.

Very truly yours,

Isaac N. Phillips

LETTER OF MR. BUNN

Springfield, Ill., Nov. 8, 1910

Isaac N. Phillips, Esq., Bloomington, Ill.

My Dear Sir: Your request that I should give you, in a letter, some of my personal recollections of Mr. Lincoln and my estimate of him, both in a social way and as a politician, is before me. My answer shall be made wholly from my personal knowledge and observation of the man. I shall, of course, not try to exhaust the subject, but will give you a little of Lincoln as I saw him and as I knew him. If, in doing this, it should appear that I put in a good deal about myself, I must plead as an excuse that I could not write my recollections of Lincoln without, to some extent, writing about myself.

I was born in Hunterdon county, New Jersey, in the year 1831. I had a brother, Jacob Bunn, who, in the year 1840, settled in Springfield, Illinois, carrying on there a wholesale and retail grocery business. In 1847, when I was in my sixteenth year, I came to live in Springfield in order to be with my brother, and I have lived at Springfield ever since. In 1847, when I came to Illinois, Lincoln had lived and practiced law at Springfield for ten years and had become somewhat distinguished throughout the State. In fact, he was then serving a term in congress from the district which included Sangamon county, Illinois. My early contact with Mr. Lincoln was brought about by the fact that he was my brother's regular attorney. Almost immediately after coming to Illinois I began to know Lincoln in such a way as a boy knows a prominent man whom he often sees and talks with.

In the year 1853,[13] I remember that Judge Douglas made a great political speech in the State House. Lincoln was present and heard him, and gave notice that he would answer Douglas, one evening very soon, from the same platform. It was a way Lincoln had to talk with people and find out the views they took of current events, but he seldom or never asked anybody's advice. Accordingly, the next day after Douglas had made his speech Lincoln came along and stopped to talk with me upon the sidewalk in front of my brother's store. He said to me, "Did you hear the speech of Judge Douglas last night?" I answered that I had heard the speech, and he said, "What do you think of it?" I replied, "Mr. Lincoln, I think it was a very

[13]1854. Douglas spoke on the afternoon of October 3, Lincoln on the afternoon of the 4th. P.M.A.

able speech, and you will have a good deal of trouble to answer it." To this he replied, "I will answer that speech without any trouble, because Judge Douglas made two misstatements of fact, and upon these two misstatements he built his whole argument. I can show that his facts are not facts, and that will refute his speech." I was present and heard the reply which Mr. Lincoln made to Judge Douglas' speech, and to my mind he did disprove Douglas' facts, and, as I thought, completely answered his arguments.

When Mr. Lincoln was elected to Congress in 1846, he was the only Whig congressman from Illinois. He served one term in congress and was not a candidate to succeed himself. After his return to private life, he was recognized as the leader of the Whig party in Illinois, just as Judge Douglas was recognized as the leader of the Democratic party in the State. These two men were the spokesmen of their respective parties, and no one disputed their supremacy. Judge Douglas soon became the leader of the Democrats of the whole North, if not of the South. These two men were leaders both in debate and in private council.

Although the Republican party first began to take form in 1854, it was not fully organized until the year 1856, when Fremont was its candidate for president. Lincoln and Douglas, as leaders of their parties, were always rivals and political antagonists. Their greatest contest was when they met as rival candidates for the Senate in the great debate of 1858. Douglas was successful and Lincoln was defeated, but the apparent defeat of Lincoln in that canvass was not a real defeat, for in that celebrated debate he laid the foundations, broad and deep, for his success over Douglas in the great presidential campaign of 1860. In the latter campaign Lincoln carried Illinois against his rival.

Lincoln was always a party man and was careful to observe and to control, within the sphere of his influence, every detail of party organization. He was always in close touch with the leaders of his party in the State. The primaries in his own ward and city, the county convention, and the State convention were each and all matters of deep personal concern to him. I do not mean that he always engaged, personally, in all the details of local campaigns, but the men who did the work were generally in his confidence, and were men who were glad to act upon his advice and suggestions. All these things were matters which Mr. Lincoln not only took pride in but enjoyed, just as any man enjoys the things that he does well and does with success.

These things, which I state as facts of my own knowledge, certainly show that Lincoln was a practical politician, but he was not altogether like many other practical politicians. He had his personal ambitions, but he never told any man his deeper plans, and few, if any, knew his inner thoughts. What was strictly private and personal to himself he never confided to any man on earth. When men have told of conversations with Lincoln in which they represent him as giving out either political or family affairs of a very sacred and secret character, their tales may be set down as false. Furthermore, Lincoln was as shrewd and unerring a judge of human nature as any man I have ever known. He understood the men about him, and he looked through and through them. If he had been going to do a thing so improbable, so contrary to his nature, as to reveal the secrets of his inmost family life to any man whatever, we may be sure his great knowledge of men would have enabled him to select someone who could be trusted not to betray his confidence to the world almost the moment his eyes closed in death.

What I have said of Lincoln's disposition to keep his own counsels does not in any way contradict the commonly accepted notion that he was a most genial man and that he was easily approachable. He was in fact a popular man with all who knew him and was generally well liked, personally, not only by his own supporters, but by the members of the party opposed to him, or at least by those members of the opposing party who were sufficiently broadminded not to be very bitter partisans.

As I have already indicated, Lincoln never, to my knowledge, sought the advice of his friends and associates as to what he should do, even in matters of great importance. However sincerely and confidently Lincoln may have worked for the success of his party, of which he was the acknowledged leader, neither his own personal interests nor the interests of his party ever, in my judgment, to any extent, controlled his political opinions or his public utterances. Lincoln may have kept many things to himself, and in many matters it may be said he was secretive, but, whenever he did speak, he said what he really thought. He never dealt in double meanings or used language for the purpose of concealing his opinions.

When, in the debate of 1858, Lincoln advanced some views, and said some things, which aroused the protests of his political associates, he was undisturbed by the criticisms that were made. It was subsequently demonstrated that he saw further and more clearly than those who accused him of ruining his own prospects and making trouble for his party. On this occasion, as on many others, in his public life, he relied on his own judgment, and his judgment proved to be correct.

Lincoln's entire career proves that it is quite possible for a man to be adroit and skillful and effective in politics without in any degree sacrificing moral principles. Little men try to do the same things he did, and make very bad work of it. They lack the high moral inspiration that animated Lincoln. Lincoln presents the most remarkable case in American history of a man who could be a practical politician and at the same time be a statesman in the highest sense of both terms. Lincoln was a high-minded patriot. He appreciated intellectual and educated men, but he was at the same time a commoner—a man of the people. He never, however, went out and told the people, in terms, that he was one of them. They knew this without any assertions of the fact. He was always ready to give his best energies and finally did give his life to the service of his country, but it is not true that he listened to the popular clamor, in order to avoid political storms, so far at least as they affected his personal interests or his political prospects. If what he said or did did not meet with popular approval he had the patience and the foresight to wait for the advance of public opinion. He did not doubt his own ability to see great situations and to solve great political and moral questions, and he always waited with perfect composure the ultimate triumph of that truth and justice which was his high and only aim.

Between 1850 and 1861, I saw Mr. Lincoln very often. I am proud to say that I was one of his junior political agents. Like very many others, I was always glad to do for him anything that I could do. I was often present at political gatherings, held for the purpose of consultation, and I thus came to know pretty well the workings of his mind, so far as they could be learned from close personal contact and observation. I certainly knew something about his personal bearing and concerning the attitude of others towards him. I never heard any man call Mr. Lincoln "Abe," and he certainly was never spoken of as "Abe" in his own presence. It was not until the campaign of 1860 that I began to hear the talk about "Abe" Lincoln and "Honest Abe." His associates always called him Mr. Lincoln. It may be that sometimes men like Judge Logan, John T. Stuart, Judge Davis or Leonard Swett, called him simply "Lincoln." His associates treated him with the respect that was due to his position, and he always behaved with dignity, so far as I observed. Many fictions of a later day have grown up about Mr. Lincoln. They are mostly exaggerations indulged in by persons who delight in telling a striking tale, and not infrequently for the purpose of making the relator seem important in his relations with Lincoln. All representations of Mr. Lincoln as a clown or a buffoon are false, and these things, to the real friends of Lincoln —men who really knew him well—are very offensive. I have always felt outraged by them.

I am also able to testify from knowledge that Mr. Lincoln was not so slovenly in his dress, and so ungainly in his appearance, as many have represented him to be. He was angular in his person, but he was agile in his movements and far less awkward in his motions than he has been represented to be. He always seemed to me to be as neat in his person and clothing as the common run of lawyers at the Western bar.

The impression has gone forth that Lincoln was always greatly embarrassed in the presence of ladies, and, indeed, that he seldom talked to ladies at all. Now, I have repeatedly seen Mr. Lincoln in social gatherings at Springfield, at the houses of prominent residents. At such places he was nearly always surrounded by ladies, who took special delight in talking to him. I did not observe his great embarrassment. I know that it may be said generally that he was as popular among women as he was among men. Women delighted to hear him talk, and he, to my certain knowledge, could talk very interestingly to them. They used to gather about him and make him talk. This was in Springfield at his home, and all I say of Lincoln is confined to the period before his departure for Washington.

In the year 1857 Mr. Lincoln asked me one day if I did not wish to run for city treasurer of Springfield. The city was then an almost hopelessly Democratic city, and the proposition rather startled me. He, however, gave me encouragement to believe that I could be elected, if I would go about the matter in the right way. My brother, Jacob Bunn, who was present at the time, said to Mr. Lincoln, "John will run if you want him to." The candidate of the Democrats was Mr. Charles Ridgely. I confess I was pleased with the idea, and, when the Republican city convention met, I was an interested auditor of the proceedings. I expected to hear my own virtues extolled in the lofty way that was common in such conventions. Lincoln had told me nothing of his plans as to how the announcement of my candidacy would be made, or in what manner I would be brought out. The convention was nearly over, and I began to think the matter of my nomination had been forgotten. In a city so Democratic as Springfield, Republican nominations were regarded at best as rather formal and perfunctory matters. Near the close of the convention a young man—a lawyer who was an inmate of Lincoln's office—addressed the chairman, and said he would like to make a nomination for the office of city treasurer, but that if the suggestion he should make did not meet with the favor of every delegate present, he would withdraw the name. He then put my name in nomination, but again said, "If there is any delegate on this floor opposed to the candidacy of Mr. Bunn, I do not wish his name to be voted upon or to go on the ticket." No one objected and I was nominated by acclamation.

When I saw who was nominating me and knew that he was an inmate of Mr. Lincoln's office, I, of course, knew very well that he was acting under Mr. Lincoln's orders. The result of the election was that I was chosen for treasurer, and, I may say, I was again chosen in 1858, in 1859 and in 1860. In all these campaigns I was, so to speak, "under the political wing" of Mr. Lincoln.

A day of two after my first nomination for city

treasurer I was going up town and saw Mr. Lincoln ahead of me. He waited until I caught up and said to me, "How are you running?" I told him I didn't know how I was running. Then he said, "Have you asked anybody to vote for you?" I said I had not. "Well," said he, "if you don't think enough of your success to ask anybody to vote for you, it is probable they will not do it, and that you will not be elected." I said to him, "Shall I ask Democrats to vote for me?" He said, "Yes, ask everybody to vote for you." Just then a well known Democrat by the name of Ragsdale was coming up the sidewalk. Lincoln said, "Now, you drop back there and ask Mr. Ragsdale to vote for you." I turned and fell in with Mr. Ragsdale, told him of my candidacy, and said I hoped he would support me. To my astonishment, he promised me that he would. Mr. Lincoln walked slowly along and fell in with me again, and said, "Well, what did Ragsdale say? Will he vote for you?" I said, "Yes, he told me he would." "Well, then," said Lincoln, "you are sure of two votes at the election, mine and Ragsdale's." This was my first lesson in practical politics, and I received it from a high source.

In the year 1861, when it was about time to nominate a treasurer again, I had a conversation with Mr. Lincoln. He asked me if I was going to run again for treasurer. I said, "Mr. Lincoln, do you not think that men frequently run for office too often for their own good?" He replied, "Yes, they very often do." I gathered from this that he probably thought I had better not run again, and so I dropped out of the race.

I may here relate a little incident which is characteristic of Lincoln. During the time between the election of Lincoln and his departure from Springfield to go to Washington, he had his office in the old State House—a building which still stands on the public square, though it has been repaired and a good deal changed. I was, of course, very greatly interested in the campaign in which the Republicans had succeeded in electing Lincoln. I was on a local committee which had charge of matters in Springfield and Sangamon county and was treasurer of the committee. One day, after the election had resulted successfully, I went up to Mr. Lincoln's room in the State House, and as I went up the stairs I met Salmon P. Chase of Ohio just coming away. When I entered the room I said to Mr. Lincoln, rather abruptly, "You don't want to put that man in your cabinet." It was an impertinent remark on my part, but Mr. Lincoln received it kindly and replied to me in a characteristic way, by saying, "Why do you say that?" Because," I said, "he

thinks he is a great deal bigger than you are."
"Well," said Lincoln, "do you know of any other
men who think they are bigger than I am?" I replied, "I do not know that I do, but why do you
ask me that?" "Because," said Mr. Lincoln, "I
want to put them all in my cabinet." This is, perhaps, unimportant talk, but I think it shows a
real characteristic of Lincoln and shows that he
was not afraid to match himself against other
men, however prominent they might be.

I always had a deep admiration and reverence
for Mr. Lincoln and, of course, was very active,
in my way, in forwarding his candidacy in the
campaign of 1860. After the campaign was over
and had been successful, I was once in Lincoln's
office in the State House, when some question
came up about my having spent a great deal of
time in and about the canvass locally. Lincoln
asked me some questions which brought out the
fact that I had spent a good deal of my own
money in the canvass—a thousand dollars, or
more. Mr. Lincoln said to me that I was not able
to lose that money. He spoke very seriously. I replied, "Yes, Mr. Lincoln, I am able to lose it, because when you go to Washington you are going
to give me an office." This statement seemed to
almost startle him. The look on his face grew
very serious. He said to me that he had not prom-

ised me any office whatever. I replied, "No, Mr. Lincoln, you have not promised me anything, but you are going to give me an office just the same." "What office do you think I am going to give you?" asked Mr. Lincoln. I said, "The office of pension agent here in Illinois. During Isaac B. Curran's term as pension agent under Buchanan I have done all the work in the office, in order to get the deposits in my brother's bank. The salary amounts to $1,000 a year, and when you go to Washington you are going to give me that office." To this he made no word of reply. He did not say he would give me the office, or that he would not, but on the 7th of March, 1861, I was appointed to the office of pension agent of Illinois by Caleb B. Smith, Secretary of the Interior.

I do not believe that anything on earth could have extracted a promise from Mr. Lincoln to give me that office, nor do I think he would have bargained to give any man an administrative office before or after his election. It is probable that he had selected the members of his cabinet, and that he had advised them of the fact before they were appointed, but, outside of his cabinet officers, I do not believe he promised anybody an office before the day of his inauguration, and yet the incident I have above related shows that he was not by any means insensible to ordinary political considerations.

Lincoln was the leading lawyer in central Illinois before his election to the presidency. He was universally respected for his purity and his uprightness and for the rigid integrity that he never failed to exhibit in all the relations of life. He received from all who came in contact with him the high respect and consideration which was due to his position and to his great ability and character.

Very truly yours,

JOHN W. BUNN

INDEX

118

Chase, Salmon P., 54; Lincoln's reasons for cabinet appointment of, 114-15
Chicago *Daily Times,* editorial excoriates Lincoln, 98-9; suppression countermanded by Lincoln, 99
Chicago, Illinois, Lincoln speaks at, 28 *n*; Lincoln-Douglas speeches, 1858, 30-1
Chitty, Joseph, studied by Lincoln, 56
Clinton, Illinois, 42
Cropsey, A. J., delegate, Republican state convention, 1860, 63
Danville, Illinois, 85
Davis, David, 45; Federal judge, 38; relations with Lincoln, 53, 109; failure to record Lincoln recollections deplored, 85-6
Decatur, Illinois, Republican state convention, 1860, 62-8, 82-3; "fence rails episode," 65-7, 82-3
Democratic Party, in Illinois, war sentiment, 1861, 86-97; ascendancy in Springfield, 1857, 111-13
Dickey, T. L., Ottawa lawyer, 22; speaks in Bloomington, 41
Douglas, Stephen A., 53; and Lincoln, on Missouri Compromise repeal, 27-8; and Lincoln speeches, 1858, 30-3, 81-2; and Lincoln's Freeport questions, 31-3; debates with Lincoln, 31-3; and Dred Scott decision, 32-3; skill and reputation as debater, 33; rejects suggestion of debates with Lincoln, 44-5; and Lincoln's "House Divided" speech, 81-2; last speech, 96-7; Lincoln and, 103-5; speech answered by Lincoln, 1853, 103-4
Dred Scott decision, in Lincoln-Douglas debates, 32-3
Ewing, James S., Lincoln Centenary speech of, 16, 37-59; biographical sketch, 36; deplores biographical misrepresentation of Lincoln, 46-9
Farnsworth, John F., speaks in Bloomington, 41
Fell, Jesse W., and Lincoln's Freeport questions, 31-2; suggests Lincoln-Douglas debates, 44-5; services to Lincoln, 45; relations with Lincoln, 53
Fitch, Henry S., United States District Attorney, Northern District of Illinois, speech quoted, 87-8
Freeport, Illinois, Lincoln-Douglas debate, 31-3
Funk, Isaac, relations with Lincoln, 53

Gagan, William, delegate, Republican state convention, 1860, 63

Gilder, Richard Watson, quoted, on Lincoln's literary style, 34-5

Gillespie, Joseph, 53; relations with Lincoln, 78-9

Gridley, Asahel, speaks in Bloomington, 41; relations with Lincoln, 53

Hamilton, Alexander, studied by Lincoln, 56

Hanks, John, "fence rails episode," Decatur convention, 65-7, 82-3

Hanna, William H., relations with Lincoln, 53

Henderson, John B., Missouri Senator, tells Lincoln story, 51-3

Herndon, William H., Lincoln law partner, quoted, estimate of Lincoln, 35

Homes, William, Illinois Democrat, speech quoted, 88

"House Divided" speech, 26-7, 30, 80-2

Illinois Central Railroad Company suit, 22

Illinois Schoolmasters' Club, 16, 37

Jarrot, Vital, member of Illinois legislature, 1861, and compromise resolutions, 93-6

Jefferson, Thomas, studied by Lincoln, 56

Lea, J. Henry and Hutchinson, J. R., *The Ancestry of Abraham Lincoln*, cited, 58-9

Legislature, Illinois, resolutions of January, 1861, 16-7, 92-6; Lincoln's election to, 1854, 28-9; elects Trumbull Senator, 29; sessions, 1861, 86 *ff*.

Lincoln, Abraham, conflicting biographical representations of, 7-10, 11, 13-18, 46-9, 59, 83-5, 100-1, 109-11; character of, 9-10, 11, 17-18, 22-3, 83-4, 106-9, 109-11, 117; had few confidants, 14, 53, 83-4, 106-8; and January 1861 resolutions of Illinois legislature, 16-17, 92-6; as story teller, 17, 23-4, 39, 50-3, 70-2; ancestry, 17-18, 56-9; qualities of leadership, 20-1, 53-4, 104-5, 106-9, 111-14, 114-15, 117; in McLean County Circuit Court, 21-2, 37-40, 69-72; intellectual superiority, 21, 53-4, 103-4, 107-9; personality, 21, 78, 83-4, 106-7, 109-11; and Illinois Central Railroad suit, 22; personal characteristics, 22-23, 65-74, 83-4, 109-11, 116-17; apostle of the common people, 24-5, 108-9; and Missouri Com-

121

ST. MARY'S COLLEGE OF MARYLAND LIBRARY
ST. MARY'S CITY, MARYLAND

37107

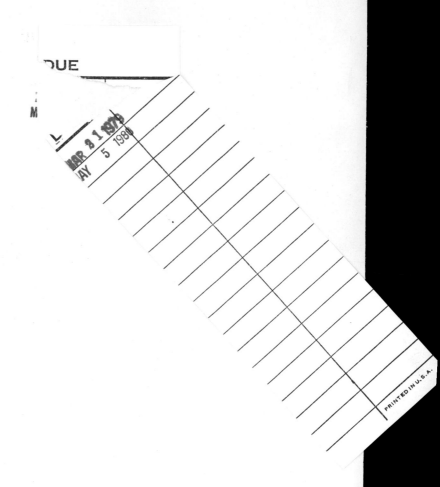